the
bridesmaid's
handbook

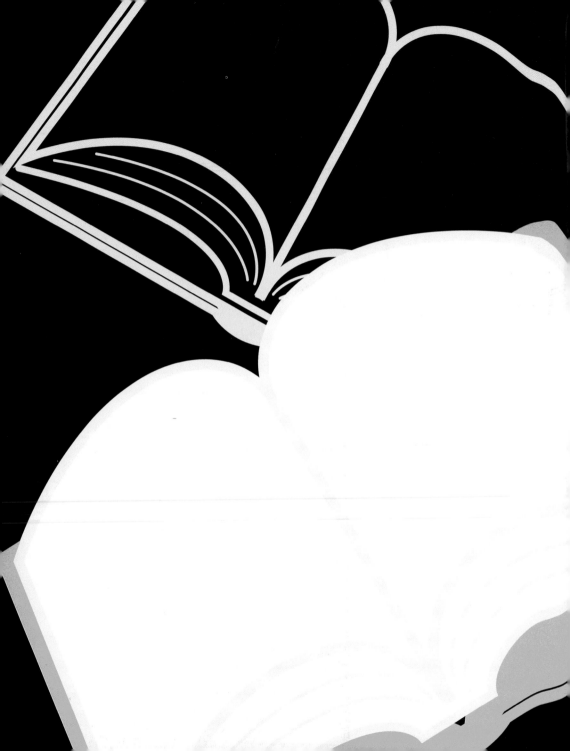

the
bridesmaid's
handbook

hamlyn

confetti.co.uk

An Hachette Livre UK company

First published in Great Britain in 2008 by
Hamlyn, a division of Octopus Publishing Group Ltd
2–4 Heron Quays, London E14 4JP
www.octopusbooks.co.uk

ISBN 978-0-600-61777-8

A CIP catalogue record for this book is available from the
British Library.

Printed and bound in China

10 9 8 7 6 5 4 3 2 1

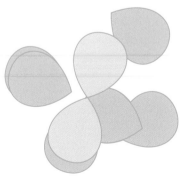

contents

Introduction

So your best friend is getting married and she's asked you to be a bridesmaid. Or perhaps it is your sister's turn to walk up the aisle and she wants you to be chief bridesmaid. Whatever your role in this big occasion – congratulations! You will no doubt be pretty elated and maybe even emotional. If you *are* going to be chief bridesmaid, you may also feel honoured to have been chosen for this pivotal role.

But what happens if this initial joy fades to fear and anxiety as you realize just what you have committed yourself to. If this is how you are feeling right now, don't worry; it is perfectly normal and this book is here to help.

Being a bridesmaid is likely to occur only once or maybe twice in your life so you'll want to do the best job you can. You will also want to prove a worthy choice for your best friend and make sure everything goes smoothly for her in the run-up to and on the big day. A chief bridesmaid has a number of 'official' duties to perform – such as organizing the hen party, keeping an eye on other attendants during the ceremony and taking on the best man for the first dance – but any bridesmaid may be called upon to perform other duties depending on the type of wedding it's going to be. Perhaps you will be consulted on choosing outfits for the attendants, asked to help organize the flowers or the cake, or to make suggestions for readings. At the very least, you will probably be needed on any number of occasions during the preparations – a moment of crisis with the reception venue, indecision over what kind of music to play or a shoulder to cry on after a family squabble – it pays to be prepared to

listen and to offer reassurance: try to be a calming influence when things start to get out of hand – which they almost certainly will.

This practical book covers everything you need to know about how you might be involved with your best friend's wedding and will be your indispensable guide in the run-up to the big day. Each chapter takes you through a key stage of your role in the wedding, offering plenty of tips and advice.

If this is the first time you've ever been a bridesmaid then you may need a little guidance. Chapter 1 outlines your duties at all stages, along with a countdown to the wedding and how you can best help. In the second chapter you'll find all the ideas and inspiration you need to organize the perfect hen party, which is one of your biggest pre-wedding jobs. One of the most important aspects for you on the big day is what will you be wearing. No need to worry as the third chapter covers everything from choosing a dress and attending fittings to who's paying and how to find the right underwear. By the time you reach Chapter 4, you'll be discovering what duties the wedding day holds in store for you, including the ins and outs of a traditional reception. And if, like an increasing number of bridesmaids, you'd like to make a speech on the big day then turn to Chapters 5, 6 and 7 which offer lots of tips on what makes a good speech, how to deliver the speech and easy to remember do's and don'ts, together with some sample snippets and sample speeches for an inspiring conclusion to the book.

For more ideas and resources, why not visit our website (www.confetti.co.uk) where you will find expert advice on your duties as chief bridesmaid or best woman and inspirational ideas for your speech.

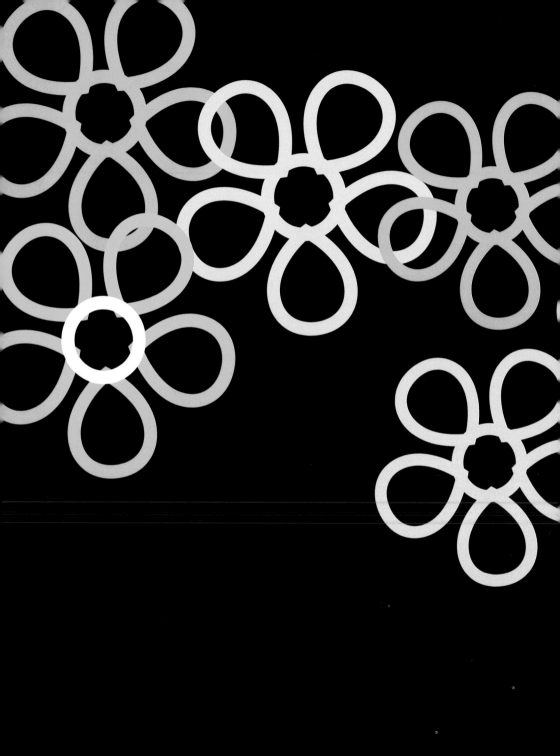

duties before the

wedding
day

Why you?

Did you know that the role of a bridesmaid dates from pagan times, when evil spirits were thought to attend wedding ceremonies? By surrounding the bride with 'look-a-likes' – similarly dressed attendants of her own age – it was thought the evil ones would not be able to single out the bride.

And, frankly, in that fuchsia taffeta horror the bride forced you into, you'd frighten the devil himself! Only kidding! Being asked to be chief bridesmaid is an honour, and most modern brides will at least let you influence the style of your dress, if not the colour.

And who needs an excuse to spend months shopping with the bride and to get totally involved in all the plans and the wedding day itself? *The Bridesmaid's Handbook* will take you through everything you need to know to be a great bridesmaid.

A band of 'sisters'

Bridesmaids are supposed to be (but are not always) unmarried. They are most often members of the bride's family: a sister, stepsister, half-sister or a favourite niece; but they can also be close friends. If the groom has a sister or a close female member of the family then it may be tactful to include her in the bridesmaids' posse.

A bride may also choose to have flower girls, page-boys and a ring bearer. But it is important for her to have at least one older attendant to help her manage these little ones on the big day.

Head girl

The chief bridesmaid is the leader of the pack and is not usually a child, since the job comes with certain duties and responsibilities. If a married woman is chosen as chief bridesmaid, then she is known by the somewhat unflattering title of matron of honour. Sometimes the most important bridesmaid is known as the best woman and she is as vital to the bride as the best man is to the groom.

If you've been chosen as chief bridesmaid, traditionally you take charge of the other bridesmaids, letting them know what to do and when to turn up to pre-wedding events such as dress fittings or the hen party.

What makes an ideal bridesmaid?

To be a good bridesmaid you need to have certain qualities – at least while you're playing the role. You should be:

- Organized – the bridesmaid is meant to look after the bride, not vice versa
- Calm – no matter what disasters might happen, you should be ready to deal with them or, at the very least, divert the bride's attention from them
- Enthusiastic – there's nothing worse than a bridesmaid who really couldn't care less
- Focused – a bridesmaid who is too busy looking after her family or chasing the best man on the day is no help at all
- Cooperative – quarrelling about the colour or cut of your own dress will only add to the overall stress
- Supportive – for those times when the napkins are the wrong shade of beige or the last pink Rolls-Royce in town is already booked.

Saying 'no'

Although it is an honour to be asked to be a bridesmaid, there are occasions when someone has to refuse. Acceptable reasons for this are:

- A prior and unmoveable engagement on that day
- A previous liaison with the groom
- An illness or disability
- A pregnancy
- You don't feel you know the bride well enough and, in fact, are unsure why she's asked you.

Unacceptable reasons for refusing, however, are:

- A burning hatred of the groom
- You don't like the dress the bride's chosen
- You get a better offer for that day
- You can't afford it.

Once you've accepted, it is essential that the bride feels that she can rely on you for moral and practical support and to share in the wedding planning. If you think you might refuse, do it straight away, before lots of money has been spent and it's too late for the bride to ask anyone else.

Your partner in crime

Where there is a wedding there is a best man and, if you have been made chief bridesmaid, it's a good idea to meet him, especially if you don't know him already. Your duties are likely to dovetail on the wedding day – at the very least, you will be required to join in the bride and groom's first dance together –

and each of you will be more confident knowing what the other is up to.

Maybe you know the best man already; chances are you have been invited to the same parties over the years, in which case he'll be a familiar face. But even if he is, it is worth calling him to talk things through and, better still, to meet up.

You don't have to present it like a date. Suggest coffee somewhere, or a light lunch/early evening drink. You can find out what else he's been asked to do, and vice versa, and you may be able to help each other out. Perhaps there are other things you could suggest doing with the best man to help the day run more smoothly – take charge of the bouquets and buttonholes or organize transport for the other bridesmaids and ushers, for example.

And then there are the hen and stag parties to sort. The best weddings are those where the primary guests get on well and are relaxed with one another. What better way to achieve this than by getting the introductions out of the way at an informal event like a joint stag and hen party?

Dress rehearsal
You'll definitely need to turn up to any wedding run-through that's been planned. This will give you a chance to familiarize yourself with the layout of the venue and get a better grasp of your role in the proceedings. Just knowing exactly where to stand and what to do on the big day will help soothe your nerves. The rehearsal may also be a good chance for you to make sure that the fees are paid in advance to all those involved in the ceremony.

Know your team

There is no harm in a bit of girl bonding before the big day. If you have been asked to be a bridesmaid, there are almost always going to be others, so why not get to know who else is involved. Perhaps the chief bridesmaid is a best friend or sister of the bride whom you've got to know well over the years and it would be good to catch up, anyway.

If you are chief bridesmaid, why not call the other girls and arrange to go out for lunch or on a girly shopping expedition together. It will be your job to make sure everyone is happy and organized on the day, so give yourself a boost by starting early and helping to make everyone feel an equal part of the show from day one. You could talk about the big day, what you might (or might not) want to wear and other ways that you could help to make the day really special. This is also a good time to discuss ideas for a hen party – whether you think the 'hen' will want to do something very quiet and low key, whether to arrange a trip abroad or whether to involve the boys, too, and have a joint hen and stag event.

And don't forget the bride – she may want to see you all together before things start to get hectic, so ask her if she would like to come along too.

Working with children

There is nothing worse than accepting to be chief bridesmaid
and then finding out that one of the attendants is the
groom's snotty 6-year-old cousin, Alfie, who blew out the
church candles at his sister's christening. If you find yourself
in such a predicament, then take a deep breath and devise a
strategy for how you are going to deal with him on the day.
It is your job to make sure young children behave in church
and are little angels for the photographs – if necessary, by
resorting to bribery. Once at the reception, you can probably
return the little monsters to their parents, but don't forget
to say nice things about them in your speech, if you are
making one.

Sister act

It is not unusual for a bride to choose a sister – either hers or
her fiancé's – to be a bridesmaid or even chief bridesmaid. If
you are a sister and chief bridesmaid, try to avoid being too
family-orientated in your approach. You almost need to make
your sister's friends your friends in order to maintain a
balance. If you are chief bridesmaid and one of the bridesmaids
is a sister to the bride or groom, you may have to tread very
carefully indeed. Chances are she is disappointed not to be in
your shoes. Try to involve her, without making it too obvious.
Above all, do not hog your friend or form a clique with other
bridesmaids who you may know (or like) better.

Know your duties

The bridesmaids play an important role at the wedding – the perfect bridesmaid should be supportive without being intrusive, helpful on the day and always available for a wedding shopping spree or for a shoulder to cry on. And, of course, there's that small matter of the hen party...

Your main duty as chief bridesmaid is to be the bride's personal assistant: someone who she can rely on to chase quotes if required or to calm her down when stress gets the better of her.

Be yourself!

An important task for any chief bridesmaid is to be an honest and reliable critic when it comes to choosing the bride's dress. Make sure she gives you some idea of what she is looking for. Then, be constructive about the styles and colours that suit her.

Along with helping the bride select her dress, the chief bridesmaid is often involved in choosing outfits for all the attendants. Ask the bride to tell you the colours and styles she is thinking of, and the ages of her attendants. You should also help coordinate the other attendants to make sure they attend dress fittings on time.

Delegating to the team, if you can

Some brides choose older bridesmaids, while others like to ask children. Whichever she chooses, you will need to help make sure they all know what is required of them and what responsibilities they may have. You can ensure everyone keeps up to speed at regular girly catch-ups or dress fittings. The more you can get the others on board the more help you'll have on the day.

Ever the diplomat

You might be asked to act as an intermediary if a difference of opinion occurs, perhaps between the bride and her parents or future parents-in-law. Fingers crossed this won't be necessary, but disagreements do happen from time to time.

Don't forget yourself!

There's nothing worse than spending all your time ensuring the bride looks beautiful and all the attendants are happy, only to discover at the last minute that your underwear is uncomfortable or you can't find your shoes.

Pre-wedding checklist

The chief bridesmaid, in particular, has a vital role in almost all preparations leading up to the day and plays a supporting role to the bride throughout the wedding day itself.

Here's a guide to what you can expect to have to do during the wedding countdown...

Six months to go

- Prepare yourself as you'll be a sounding board for the bride's ideas right from the start. You'll need to research ideas for all sorts of things – from flowers and cakes to outfits and make-up.
- This is a good time to organize a girly day out to get everyone in the mood.
- Book accommodation, if necessary, at the venue or nearby so you don't have a long journey home after the wedding.

Four months to go

- Support the bride in every way possible – if she is trying out a new beauty regime or has taken up jogging, try to go along too, to keep up morale.
- Arrange a makeover with a professional. Having a makeover is a fun way to spend a morning or afternoon. Try out some new brands or make-up artists for the big day and see what suits you, or just enjoy yourselves doing something girly.
- Check that the bride's other attendants have made the necessary arrangements for their outfits, and that they know when the rehearsals or dress fittings are.
- Get together with the other bridesmaids and start to think about the hen party. Check out the ideas in Chapter 2 (see pages 32–53).

Two months to go

- Get the bride to give you everyone's contact details of those she'd like to come to her hen do.
- Contact all her friends and book a date for the hen party; then decide on the event, venue and theme.
- Start to think about whether you're going to make a speech (at the hen party or bridal shower). Or perhaps you're going to say a few words at the wedding itself.
- Research material for the speech. You'll find plenty of ideas and material in the Speech Centre on our website (www.confetti.co.uk) and in Chapters 5, 6 and 7 (see pages 100–157).
- Encourage the bride (not that she'll probably need much encouragement!) to start a course of facials, manicures and pedicures so she will look her best on the day. (And of course, you'll benefit as well...)
- Book a back-to-back appointment with her hairdresser so you can both try out wedding hairdos.
- Offer words of calm and support for the bride, especially if she's been taken over by 'Bridezilla' (see page 150). *The Confetti Wedding Book of Calm* might be just the thing to give her, for last-minute tips on staying frazzle-free.

One week to go

- Attend the wedding rehearsal (if you're chief bridesmaid, at least) so that you know exactly where you and other attendants should stand, when you should sit down and the order of the ceremony, especially if you're doing a reading.
- Toast the couple at the dinner after their wedding rehearsal, it's a tradition for you to do this.
- Phone all the other attendants to make sure no one's suffering from last-minute nerves or problems that they're too embarrassed to speak to the bride about.
- Check with the best man to see how the 'other side' is holding up.
- Collect together your outfit, including underwear and shoes, and hang it up in a safe place along with a small bag with your make-up for the day; if you're making a speech and need prompts, then make sure you leave a printout here too. Then you can relax... well sort of.

How you might help

Not all weddings are traditional in the sense that the parents of the bride foot the bill for everything, or that all of the arrangements are made by close members of the family alone. In the case of older couples, second-time brides or weddings where the bride and groom are financially independent, it is not unusual for the bride and groom to do much of the organizing themselves.

If this is the case for you, then the bride and groom may have a lot of things to think about and a tremendous amount of planning to do. And this is where you come in; this is not just the domain of the chief bridesmaid, either. In fact, the chief bridesmaid will probably have enough to deal with organizing the hen party, so helping out in the following ways could be something for any of the bridesmaids. Have a think about whether you would like to offer help and what you might like to do. Here are just a few ideas:

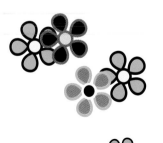

- Help with the flower arrangements – The bride might welcome your thoughts on colour schemes for the flowers, and names of reputable local florists. Depending on the type of wedding, you might offer to help make bouquets and table decorations or to book the florist/oversee delivery (see pages 22–25).
- Take charge of the cake arrangements – If the bride is having a cake made, you could offer to ensure its safe delivery at the reception venue and organize payment (a cheque on the day is usually fine). If you're a domestic goddess, you could even offer to make the cake yourself (see pages 26–27).

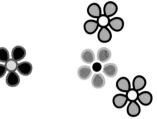

- Organize and coordinate dress fittings – You could liaise with the bride/chief bridesmaid and other attendants to make sure that everyone is in the right place at the right time.
- Suggest some readings – If there are going to be readings at the ceremony, you could research some and put forward some suggestions; you could also offer to read something yourself (see pages 28–31).
- Look after the wedding list – Taking charge of the gift list could take a weight off the bride's mind.
- Follow the bride's new regime – If the bride is determined to get into shape for the big day, you could join her on this new fitness quest.

And in addition to those pre-wedding duties, there are various responsibilities you can take on after the big day (see pages 98–99).

Don't over-commit!
A word of warning:

- Your offer must be genuine: the bride will be relying on you to make sure certain aspects of her wedding go off without a hitch. You must be prepared to give your all.
- Do not overcommit yourself: try to confine yourself to just one or two tasks, particularly if you are the chief bridesmaid and also have the hen party to worry about.
- Be diplomatic: if the bride's parents are involved, particularly financially, their opinions must also be considered.

- The bride's say is final: you may have great ideas, but you must be prepared to pander to her wishes (even when she changes her mind for the fifth time).
- Keep a record: even the best-laid plans can go wrong, especially when there are many people involved. Make sure you keep track of any arrangements you are responsible for and, above all, keep the bride informed and up to date.

Organizing flowers

Helping decide on the flowers for the wedding needs to be done at about the same time as the transport is arranged – at least six months before the wedding. Offer the bride a range of floral ideas so that she can choose varieties to complement the style of her day. There's lots to organize in terms of flower arrangements so offering to take on this job, if you can, will help out greatly.

Traditionally, the groom pays for the bride's bouquet, buttonholes, corsages and the flowers for the bridesmaids, while the bride's parents pay for the ceremony and reception flowers. When researching costs, remember to get a written quotation from florists well in advance and make sure that it covers all the extras, including floral headdresses and thank-you bouquets for the mothers, if you're having them.

Whatever flowers the bride decides on, try to steer her to keep the arrangements to scale with the venue and occasion. A grand wedding requires more stylized floral arrangements, while a small reception at home could be adequately catered for with simple vase arrangements and bunches of flowers.

Flowers for the wedding party

The bride usually carries a bouquet and wears flowers in her hair or a 'crown' of flowers to hold her veil in place. One thing to bring to the bride's attention is that flowers for buttonholes, corsages and hair should be wired or preserved (to prevent them from wilting), which may influence her choice one way or the other.

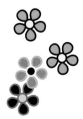

The bride's flowers set the tone and scheme for the bridesmaids' bouquets, the buttonholes for the groom, best man, ushers and father of the bride, and the corsages for the couple's mothers. The tradition of a flower girl strewing petals along the aisle is very sweet, but check first that the officiant at the church, register office or venue approves.

Finding a florist

Ask the bride if she has a budget. She will probably have a ballpark figure by now and so do some research to make sure this is realistic. You may well be surprised at how much flowers cost.

Next, you need to see if the bride has anyone in the family or a close friend who could take on the floristry arrangements or whether a professional florist is the way to go. If you don't already have a florist or a skilled family member in mind, ask everyone local to the venue for recommendations. Standards of service vary considerably. Always ask to see photos of other wedding flower arrangements that the florist has done.

The price of flowers can be alarming and much depends on seasonal availability, so if the bride's budget is looking tight then find out what's in season and work round it. When visiting a florist, take as much information with you as you can. If possible, take sketches of the bride's dress, the attendants' clothes and samples of the fabrics. You could also cut out pictures from magazines of the kinds of bouquet the bride particularly likes. All this will help the florist achieve the best possible result for the special day. A good florist will also ask to visit the church or register office and the reception venue if you've hired them to decorate those too.

Flowers for each event

Different venues require different levels of floral arrangement. So, depending on where the wedding is going to be, accompany the bride on visits to get an idea of what level of flowers is needed.

Church flowers

The most usual positions for flower arrangements are on the chancel steps, the windowsills and the pew-ends. Some clergymen will allow the altar to be decorated, while others are strongly opposed to the idea.

The bride may be happy to leave floral decorations to those who arrange the church flowers every week. The advantage of this is that they know where flowers show to the best advantage. However, if the bride is not happy with this arrangement, it may be possible to negotiate – after all, she'll be paying for the flowers and most probably the arranger, too.

Find out if another wedding service is taking place on the same day as the bride's. If so, it makes sense for the brides (or chief bridesmaids) to contact each other and perhaps arrange to share the cost. Why not suggest the bride gives the venue flowers to a local hospital or old people's home after the ceremony (and usually after the Sunday service is over)? The flowers will last for a week or so, and that way many people benefit from her day.

Flowers at a register office

Many register offices change their flowers daily. However, if the bride wants to have a special arrangement, prompt her to speak to the registrar about it, sooner rather than later.

Reception flowers

Flower arrangements are very much determined by the venue and the formality (or not) of the reception. It's nice for guests waiting in line to see an arrangement of flowers nearby. Other arrangements can be placed around the hall or marquee. Smaller displays on individual tables add an air of festivity and charm.

If a hall or rooms are being hired for the reception, flowers are sometimes included in the package. If this is the case at the reception venue, then check yourself or make sure that the bride will like them and that they match her colour scheme. Again, if there is another wedding the day before or the day after then the bride might be able to share the costs with another bride.

Many couples prefer to use fresh flowers to adorn their wedding cake rather than artificial ones. So, if you're dealing with the cake, bear this in mind when looking at ordering numbers with the florist and/or the bride.

The bride's bouquet

The style of the wedding dress and colours of the wedding party are the most important aspects to be considered when choosing a bridal bouquet. There are many different types available, from a wild flower posy to a single amazing lily stem. Some brides even choose a freeze-dried bouquet, which lasts forever.

After the wedding, if the bride would like her bouquet preserved make sure you take it somewhere safe and keep it watered and cool. Many companies preserve fresh flower bouquets, and will give instructions on what to do after the big day to keep them in their best state.

Matching the season
These days you can find almost any kind of flower at any time of the year, but if you want to keep costs down suggest something to suit the season of the bride's wedding.

Spring – Daffodils, narcissi, bluebells, freesias, tulips and hyacinths.

Summer – Roses, hydrangeas, stephanotis, lisianthus, sunflowers, sweet peas, delphiniums and larkspur.

Autumn – Chrysanthemums, wheat, euphorbia, hypericum berries, alstroemeria and gerbera.

Winter – Ivy, lilies, orchids, hippeastrum, dark red roses and dendrobium.

The cake

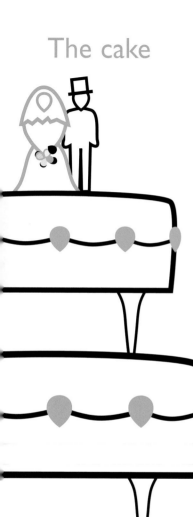

Not all weddings have a wedding cake, but it is traditional for the couple to formally 'cut' the cake while everyone looks on and cheers. In fact, it is an age-old symbol of fertility.

The traditional wedding cake is a rich fruit cake with thick icing. It's usually square or round and comes in two or three tiers. But there's nothing to stop the bride choosing something completely different (see right).

Who will make the cake?

As with the flowers, knowing what the options are will help you offer the bride suitable choices when it comes to the cake. Quiz her, too, on whether she favours the traditional wedding cake tier or if she wants to go 'off piste' and design her own?

The various options for the cake are:
- Buy a standard cake and have it specially decorated
- Have it made by a specialist
- Have it made by a relative or friend and then iced professionally
- Have it made and iced by a relative or friend
- Order it from your local bakery.

Ordering the cake

Make sure that the bride is aware of the fact that she'll need to order the wedding cake in good time – a multi-tiered cake can take months to create and it will need to be made and iced in different stages. Flowers generally form the main cake decorations (whether real, fabric or piped in icing), although some couples like to include balloons, ribbons or horseshoes and figurines.

It is best for the cake to be delivered to the reception venue unassembled and then the tiers put together *in situ*. Make sure the venue has somewhere safe to store the cake and that they can assemble it for you.

If some cake is going to be sent out to guests that can't make the wedding day – an old custom that is often upheld at traditional weddings – you will need names and addresses for these people in advance of the wedding.

Bucking the trend

If the bride can't abide fruit cake and the groom just won't give in to a chocolate cake, there isn't a problem. There are lots of alternatives.

- Try a wedding trifle, everyone loves the layers.
- Think old-fashioned tea party. Buy some interesting moulds and serve up platefuls of jelly and ice cream.
- What about a *croquembouche?* This traditional French wedding cake is made from profiteroles and glazed with caramel.
- Have a traditional-looking cake with a choice of different fillings. But bear in mind that the top layer should be made of sponge as the lightest layer needs to go on the top.
- Why not go for a gloriously summery wedding pavlova? With mango, strawberries and lashings of double cream, what could be yummier?
- Go for a designer dessert – cake designers can make wonderful novelty cakes, which are particularly good for themed weddings.
- Treat everyone's tastebuds to the sheer indulgence of a chocolate fountain.
- Hire an ice-cream van if the wedding is happening on a beach.
- Instead of one large cake, why not have lots of little cup cakes iced in white with flowers on top, or in blue for the groom and pink for the bride?

Readings

One way that you can contribute to the day is by offering to read a passage at the wedding ceremony, whether it is in a church or in a register office. Giving a reading brings some sentiment into the service and ensures it is a day to remember, particularly if you have known the bride for a long time, know the groom very well too or are a sister as well as a bridesmaid. It's not solely the domain of the chief bridesmaid, any bridesmaid can offer to read. It will help you to feel you are making a valuable contribution to the bride's big day without stealing anyone's thunder.

The most likely time for readings is between the wedding vows and the signing of the register. This is the same for both church and civil weddings. In some cases, there might also be a reading at the beginning of the wedding ceremony or just before everyone leaves to go to the reception.

If you are giving a reading you will want to make sure it is appropriate, not just for the occasion, but also for who you are and your relationship to the bride and groom. Obviously love makes for good subject matter, but you can also seek out readings that discuss loyalty, friendship, trust, happiness and unity. There is a wealth of material to consider when choosing something to read, but you do need to bear in mind a few guidelines.

- For a church wedding, your bride and groom might prefer a biblical reading rather than something secular. Although secular readings are acceptable, you may have to seek the approval of the priest or vicar for any you choose.
- For a civil wedding, the choice is unlimited in terms of secular material, but you cannot have any religious texts. All readings must gain the approval of the registrar.
- For a humanist wedding, you have much more flexibility and can choose readings of any kind.

Typical order of service
- Bride enters
- Introduction by officiator
- Reading (optional)
- The marriage
- Sermon/hymns (church wedding)
- Readings
- Signing of the register
- Reading (optional)
- Exit

A selection of readings

Familiarize yourself with the following readings to get
yourself in the right frame of mind for choosing a reading.

Readings for a church ceremony

Two are better than one
9 Two are better than one, because they have a good
return for their work:
10 If one falls down, his friend can help him up. But pity the
man who falls and has no one to help him up.
11 Also, if two lie down together, they will keep warm. But
how can one keep warm alone?
12 Though one may be overpowered, two can defend
themselves.
Ecclesiastes 4:9–12

Wedding prayer
Robert Louis Stevenson (1850–1894)

Lord, behold our family here assembled.
We thank you for this place in which we dwell,
for the love that unites us,
for the peace accorded us this day,
for the hope with which we expect the morrow,
for the health, the work, the food,
and the bright skies that make our lives delightful;
for our friends in all parts of the earth.
Amen

Readings for a civil ceremony
A good wedding cake (Author unknown)

4lb of love
½lb of good looks
1lb of sweet temper
1lb of butter of youth
1lb of blindness of faults
1lb of wit
1lb of good humour
2 tablespoons of sweet argument
1 pint of laughter
1 wine glass of common sense
dash of modesty

Put the love, good looks and sweet temper into a well-furnished house. Beat the butter of youth to a cream and mix well together with the blindness of faults. Stir the wit and good humour into the sweet argument, then add laughter and common sense. Add a dash of modesty and work together until everything is mixed. Bake gently for ever.

The day (Author unknown)
May this be the start of a happy new life that's full of special moments to share
May this be the first of your dreams come true and of hope that will always be there...
May this be the start of a lifetime of trust and of caring that's just now begun...
May today be a day that you'll always remember the day when your hearts become one...

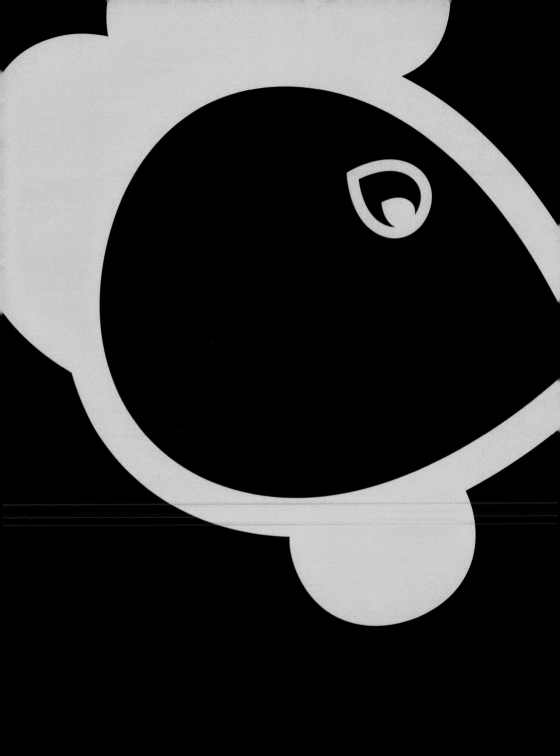

the
hen
party

Organizing the hen party

It's up to you, and the other bridesmaids, to organize the hen party, the bride's traditional farewell to single life. In preparing your send-off, resist the pressure to live up – or down – to the abundance of hen-night horror stories. Ultimately this event is an affectionate celebration, rather than a gruesome ordeal of initiation. And today's hen 'do's are all about originality and style.

Traditionally, the hen is kept in the dark about her hen do, but it's probably a good idea to discuss with her what sort of celebration she wants. Get planning and get creative. First, you need to find out exactly who she wants to invite and compile a guest list. For example, does she want to include work colleagues and parents or just make it a smaller group of close friends? Think about the group's ages and interests – different activities throughout the day may need to be organized, for example, go-karting for all, after which parents and the younger contingent can leave while the big girls go clubbing.

Get the hen to give you the contact details for everyone she wants to invite and try to get in touch with everyone to set a date six to eight weeks in advance of the approximate date, to maximize the chances of everyone being free at the same time. Remember, this is your opportunity to take charge and concoct a memorable event for the bride and the other bridesmaids in the party, so don't leave things to chance. You can make the difference between just another night in the pub and a legendary send-off – and no, it's not down to your karaoke performance of *My Way*.

Bridal showers

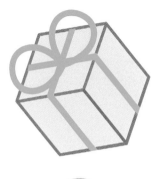

These American-inspired events are gaining popularity in the UK and make a refreshing alternative to the booze-fuelled trawl of the local haunts. Traditionally, a shower is held at the bride's (or close relative's) house a fortnight or so before the wedding. Immediate female relatives of both the bride and the groom are invited, as well as close girl friends, and arrive bearing gifts with which to 'shower' the bride. Snacks and party games ensue and a girly good time is had by all.

As with hen parties, the event is usually organized by the chief bridesmaid and the bride is quite often in on the arrangements. In fact, if this is the route you want to go down, it is a good idea to make sure it appeals to the bride before going too far with your arrangements, even if it is supposed to be a secret. Try dropping some helpful hints to get a rough idea of what she would like to do. If she's expecting a trip to Ibiza you are probably wasting your time.

A good way to proceed is to focus the event on one or two of your bride's particular interests. Pick something she really loves doing as a theme for the party. This way you give the guests some direction on the sort of thing they can bring as a gift.

Five top bridal shower ideas

- For a girl who loves to be pampered – Hire a beautician or masseur (or a team of them) for the day and indulge the bride and guests with manicures, pedicures and massages. Cosmetics and toiletries make ideal gifts.
- For a glamour puss – Have a cocktail night: posh frocks, barman and all. Or have a hot-tub in the garden with a butler to cook delicious nibbles throughout the event and serve champagne (some even clear up afterwards!). Gifts could include exquisite trinkets, pretty accessories and the like.
- If she likes a night in – Arrange a sleepover and hire some soppy films. Ideal gifts include DVDs of favourite films, CDs of film soundtracks, a box of tissues...
- For a bride who loves her food – Book a chef for an evening and have him or her prepare a lavish buffet. Guests can shower the bride with fine wines and chocolates.
- For a girl who likes to be entertained – Find a magician/clown/comedian who puts on a good show. Friends can shower the bride with fireworks for a grand finale; this works best if you have quite a big crowd.

Etiquette corner
It is customary for the chief bridesmaid to give a speech at a bridal shower, which could be a blessing in disguise, saving you from having to make one at the wedding. You'll want to do your best for a speech, whenever you give one, so check out Chapters 5, 6 and 7 for top tips on writing and giving a speech along with masses of speech material.

When and where to hold a hen party

Nowadays, the night before the wedding is considered a definite no-no for the hen party. The best time is at least a week (and preferably two or more) before the big day and, if possible, over the same weekend as the groom's stag do – this means the couple won't lose two weekends together in the crucial last few planning weeks before the wedding.

You'll also need to think about the party location. Do most of the guests live in the same area or is there a central town that's easily accessible for everyone?

Cash-wise, everyone generally pays for themselves and then chips in to cover the bride, too. It's less hassle to ask everyone to contribute towards a kitty before you go out.

If you're spending a weekend away, send everyone a note or email asking for a cheque in advance to cover their costs. Make it clear that unless they pay up you can't reserve their place.

Places to go

As if anyone needs an excuse for a weekend away, hen parties offer the ultimate reason. But do bear in mind who's coming to the event. Trips abroad can be costly and this may exclude some of the girls who'd love to join the party, so don't go overboard.

- Weekends abroad – with cheap flights, Paris, Brussels, Barcelona and Rome are hot destinations for hens and stags. You could try to time it around a local festival, exhibition or sporting event.

- Activity days – go-karting or sports car driving, abseiling and other outdoor activities are all great options for team building and a memorable day.

Get organized

As soon as you know the who, when and where you really ought to get going. Your computer will be a true friend for this task, and the revolution that is email has made organizing hen parties, and any big gatherings, so much simpler. Enlist help if you need to or find the organization is swamping you. The last thing you want is to have your bride chasing you on this, and you cannot afford to let her down by leaving it all too late. Give the girls plenty of advance warning and nail each one for a genuine commitment (expect this to be tricky with the ones who know the bride, but none of her other girl friends).

You'd be surprised how difficult it can be to rally a troop of girls for an event like this, so here are a couple ideas to help smooth the way:

- Make sure you get an address, phone number and email details for each girl to be invited.
- Send out formal invitations four to six weeks before the hen party – having something tangible to reply to often gets a good response.
- Chase no-response invitees two weeks after the first invite and weekly thereafter.
- Enlist the help of one or two other bridesmaids in chasing up people.

Holding a joint hen and stag do

While still very much the non-traditional option, some couples opt to have a joint hen and stag party, particularly if they have known each other for a long time and all their friends are well acquainted. If you are planning one, make sure it's not going to cause problems for couples with children who might have difficulty getting someone to look after the kids.

It is unlikely that such an event will be a secret from the bride and the groom – there are simply too many variables. So, as chief bridesmaid, you might want to get together with the happy couple and the best man to see what will work best. Remember that you have to appeal to more people with this option – and to both sexes – so it can often involve a fair amount of work.

Your main options are organizing a day out together, a night on the town, or a weekend away. You could even split the event so that you are together as one group during the day, but have separate hen and stag activities in the evening. Either way it is best to have a clear focus to prevent the event becoming just another great shindig with your best mates. Here are some ideas.

A day out together

- Opt for something active. Paintballing, go-karting, bungee-jumping, sailing or dry-slope skiing are all great fun and reasonably priced when done en masse.
- Organize a trip to a sporting event – a favourite football team's match in winter or a day at the races for a fine summer's day, with picnic and fizz to boot.

- Have a day out at a theme park. Alton Towers, Lightwater Valley and Blackpool Pleasure Beach have some fantastic rollercoasters.

A night on the town

- Organize a good, old-fashioned night down the pub. Find one that has a quiz night, a dartboard, pool and/or karaoke.
- Book a group ticket for a night of comedy, a great play or a favourite band.
- Dance the night away at a club with Latin dancing or head for the nearest 70s disco night.

A weekend away

- Organize a city break: Dublin, Amsterdam and Paris are all top locations.
- Get in touch with the Landmark Trust and find a castle, fort or folly to stay in.
- B&B it by the sea for a weekend of donkey rides, candyfloss and the penny arcades.

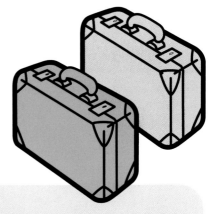

Joint ventures

Before you get too carried away, here are a few tips on running a joint event:

- Have a very clear idea of budget and number of guests.
- Divide responsibilities between you and the best man, make sure you are both clear on who is organizing what.
- Be realistic in what you can achieve in a night, day or weekend. Do not pick an evening event that requires lots of travel.

On the day or night

It's your responsibility to look after the bride and make sure she gets home in one piece. If the celebrations include activities or alcohol, don't let the bride attempt to do anything or drink any more than she could normally cope with on a night out.

Your main challenge is to keep the momentum going, so try to pace the events. If lots of alcohol is involved, don't let everyone – especially not the bride! – drink too much too soon. Planning a meal in a restaurant as part of the celebrations or organizing food to be laid on in a pub will help with this.

A sight for sore eyes

Take a camera with you to record the various activities of the memorable event, or a video camera to capture all the live action. Polaroids have a timeless quality and are fun to take; you could assemble a hen party diary with the polaroids in a special album and present them to the bride at the reception on her wedding day. What a fantastic souvenir! Disposable cameras also work well and are available to buy at numerous shops and also on the internet, for instance, at www.confetti.co.uk.

Paying up

The costs should be divided among the group – the bride shouldn't have to pay for anything. If a pub crawl is planned, the money needs to be sorted out before people get too carried away – it's a good idea for everyone to be asked to contribute towards a kitty at the start of the evening, and it is topped up as necessary as the night goes on. If it's an action day or weekend away that involves making a group booking, a note/email can be sent in advance to everyone taking part asking for a cheque to cover costs. The best man or chief bridesmaid should make it clear to the guests that unless they pay up their places can't be reserved.

A night to remember

Evening activities for a group of hens are plentiful and are particularly suited to a larger gathering. Depending on budget and taste you can arrange anything from a fancy meal at a top restaurant to taking in a West End show. A night on the town is also quite a good idea if you have trouble getting a few guests to commit; most events are pay as you go, so you will avoid the issue of covering someone else's costs if they don't show up.

A meal out

Plenty of hens like the idea of going to a swish restaurant for their hen do. If you have a large group of girls, ask every other guest to move a couple seats to the left with each new course to mix things up a bit and so you get to meet everyone else. Another great idea is to have each course in a different restaurant (remember to make this clear to the restaurants when you make your bookings, though). Before choosing your restaurant it is a good idea to check your guests' dietary requirements – you don't want to turn up at a steak house with three vegans in your midst.

Dance away

The informality of a club or disco is perfect for a hen party that involves lots of girls, especially if some of them can make it only for an hour or so. Pick a venue that is easy to get to and that has cheapish accommodation nearby for anyone who wants to party into the early hours. For the die-hard

clubbers, it could be good fun to see if you can get on the guest list at one of the more exclusive venues.

Cocktail heaven

Who can resist the glamour of the cocktail bar? Find one with real swank and invite all the girls to come dressed for the part. Before embarking on your night of chinking glasses among the sequins and pearls, however, remember that cocktails can be really pricey. Plenty of bars have a 2-for-1 happy hour and you may want to time your visit to coincide with that – so what if it is at 5pm!

Take in a show

You could opt for a night at the movies – maybe seek out a Woody Allen double bill or a horror film night at the local indy cinema. An alternative is to make a group booking at the local comedy club or fringe theatre. Perhaps your bride has always wanted to see *Les Miserables* or *We Will Rock You* (there's no accounting for taste). Whatever you end up doing, make sure there is plenty of time either before or after – preferably both – for a few drinks and lots of chatting.

The perfect day-trip

If your bride is unlikely to fancy a night on the tiles, then organizing a great day out could be the answer. Consider your bride's personal tastes – would she like to do something cultural, something relaxing or have a once-in-a-lifetime experience? Anything is possible. There are options for groups of any size and a day out can often be less costly than an evening event.

A spot of culture

If your bride is the cultured kind, organize a day out around an art exhibition, poetry reading or book launch. You could meet for coffee beforehand and have a late lunch or afternoon tea afterwards. If that does not appeal, seek out one of the museums or galleries in your area, or for outdoors types spend a day at Kew Gardens or The Eden Project.

A day at a health spa

If a bit of luxury is called for, you cannot beat a day of pampering – it's every girl's dream. Check in for a full day's worth of indulgence, including lunch and a few treatments. That way it is up to each guest to spend as much (or as little) as she likes, without feeling self-conscious. Some spas have offers for groups and overnight stays, so shop around for the best deals.

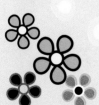

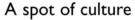

Having a flutter

Who says you have to go out at night to get dressed up?
If it's a summer do then Ladies' Day at Ascot is the perfect
excuse for pushing the boat out, or if the timing's not
quite right a day at the races can do just as well. Have a
competition to see who can wear the most outrageous hat
with the greatest style. It is impossible not to get swept up
in the atmosphere – drinking champagne all the way, and
placing the odd bet on the horses. Someone might even
win some money!

Parlez-vous francais?

The thrill of travel without the expense (depending on how
you do it). There are countless cheap offers for day trips to
France, either by ferry or by train. These generally involve a
Dover–Calais crossing or Dover–Boulogne. If you plan literally
to get off the boat, have lunch, do some hypermarket shopping
and come back (all respectable day-trip-to-France activities)
opt for Boulogne, which is a far prettier destination than
Calais. Those on a bigger budget, should get on Eurostar for a
return trip to Lille or even Paris – possible (just) in a day.

A weekend break

Although there is no reason why you cannot organize a weekend away for a large group of girls, for many reasons these are better suited to a smaller group – say somewhere between five and eight. Not only are you likely to run into various logistical problems with a larger group (dietary considerations, room sharing, transport), there are also bound to be one or two guests who do not know each other very well. Spending a weekend away with strangers may not be their cup of tea, particularly if some of you are quite cliquey. Also, bear in mind that a weekend break can be expensive, so you want to make sure everyone is totally committed before making any costly bookings.

Camping out

This is a great option if your bride and the rest of the hens are outdoorsy types. Given the British climate, you will want to choose a weekend when there is less chance of rain (not always easy, even in summer). Get it right and you can have a relaxing couple of days with country walks, pub lunches and singing round the campfire. Better still, if a number of you are seasoned campers, there is a chance that you'll have enough equipment between you to make this a relatively cheap option.

A cottage in the country

If camping is not quite the bride's style, you can still have the country walks and pub lunches, but with the comfort of a proper roof over your heads when it comes to bedtime. This is a real treat in autumn or winter, when you can cook up big roast dinners and have the log fire burning, while you tell each other gruesome stories or hark back to the good-old school-days. Check out the Landmark Trust for houses with architectural interest, an unusual twist or a bit of local history.

A city break

If you are a small group and are prepared to spend a little more money on your bride's hen party, consider a weekend in Paris, Rome, Lisbon or Barcelona. All destinations are easy to get to, and you are guaranteed to have a couple of days glamour shopping, gourmet eating, and as much culture as you want. You need to be well organized, though, if you want to make the most of your time abroad and, although it sounds daft, it makes sense to do a bit of reading and research and to have some kind of an itinerary. A city break does not have to happen over the weekend, and you might find some good mid-week deals, work permitting.

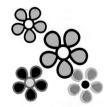

A week's holiday

For a close group of friends, a proper holiday can be the best way to celebrate your bride's hen party, and more and more hens are taking this option. It offers a great opportunity for reminiscing over past girly times together and plenty of time for speculating over the future. Time it well and you could also be tanned and beautiful for the big day. This approach will suit only a handful of girls prepared to commit both time and money, however. If you're asking working girl friends to sacrifice a chunk of their annual leave to boot, don't be too surprised if a couple of them decline to come along.

A cheap package

If there are not too many of you – say a maximum of four – and all you want is a week of lazy sunshine, why not wing it and try to snap up a last-minute booking to a Spanish Costa, a Greek island or the Red Sea? There are plenty of deals to be had, almost all year round, and you should be spoilt for choice. This way you can pick up a bargain at relatively short notice and have the thrill of not knowing your destination until you are practically boarding the plane!

High-glamour clubbing

If your bride knows what she wants, and what she wants is clubbing at its best, you are wasting your time if you look anywhere other than Ibiza. The original clubbers' paradise, this stunning island is still hard to beat for lolling around on the beach by day and getting sucked into the frantic world of top-end clubs by night. If you are looking for full-on and frenetic, this is definitely your bag.

The big chill

This could be the answer if a day at the spa is simply not enough. There are a number of truly amazing spa resorts in Europe, and many offer deals so it is worth doing your homework. For the ultimate experience book into the Blue Lagoon in Iceland or Budapest's Gellert Bath and Spa, where the surroundings themselves are to die for. In addition to bathing in natural thermal pools, there are countless relaxing treatments to choose from, including massages, saunas, mud packs and steam baths.

Mega blow out

If you are spending money, you might as well spend a lot and what better destination for blowing cash than Las Vegas (you don't even need a week to empty your bank account)? Bright lights and whirring machines are all part of the action here, where you can hit the floor of many a casino, trying your luck at craps, blackjack, baccarat and poker. You can get some great deals for all-in trips that include flight, hotel and food. This is not a trip the bride will forget in a hurry – just make sure you are not upstaging the groom with the honeymoon.

Make it personal

If you are arranging a special event with some of the bride's closest friends and relatives, you are probably doing enough to make the hen party a personal and memorable experience. Some like to add a couple of finishing touches, however, and you will have seen many a bride wearing devil's horns or sporting an L-plate to mark the occasion. Visit www.confetti.co.uk/shopping for inspiration.

There are various ways in which you can personalize the bride's hen party. For example, you could have T-shirts printed for all of the guests or ask them to come in fancy dress. If you are having a night in town, you could hire a limousine to get you from one venue to the next (and home). Buy some disposable cameras and ask the guests to take turns shooting the party as it unfolds, then present the bride with an album sometime later as a souvenir.

Theme it

If fancy dress appeals, make sure it is a suitable option for the occasion. It is fine (ish) if you are going out for a meal or going clubbing, but somehow less appropriate for go-karting or tea at the Ritz. If you are having a joint hen and stag do choose a complementary theme for the boy and girl groups: villains and heroes; tarts and vicars; doctors and nurses is the way to go.

Hen party checklist

Don't let the logistics spoil your celebrations. To make sure everything goes well, have a definite plan and stick to it. Here's a handy list to help you remember what to do:

- Draw up a list of people to invite, in consultation with the bride. And make sure you have all their contact details.
- Select a town/venue that's easily accessible to everyone.
- Decide on what kind of hen party would be best for the people involved, establish an itinerary and make enquiries, and then some provisional bookings.
- Pre-book everything you can so you're not thwarted by not being able to get into a venue/restaurant. Confirm bookings in writing (especially accommodation) and reconfirm the day before by phone, too.
- Let invitees know well in advance if there's anything extra they should bring along with them – such as props, funny stories about the bride/groom, old photos, a change of clothes – and be contactable to answer any queries.
- Create and send out invitations.
- Make sure that everyone knows exactly where you're meeting. Give a contact number – ideally a mobile phone number – for any last-minute changes/confirmations.
- Make sure everyone knows roughly how much the do will cost – and that they'll be helping to cover the bride's costs. Let everyone know when payment should be made.
- Have a fall-back meeting place for late arrivals/people who get lost.
- Find out how everyone will get back home. Do you need to arrange transport/book taxis/send younger members of the party home earlier?

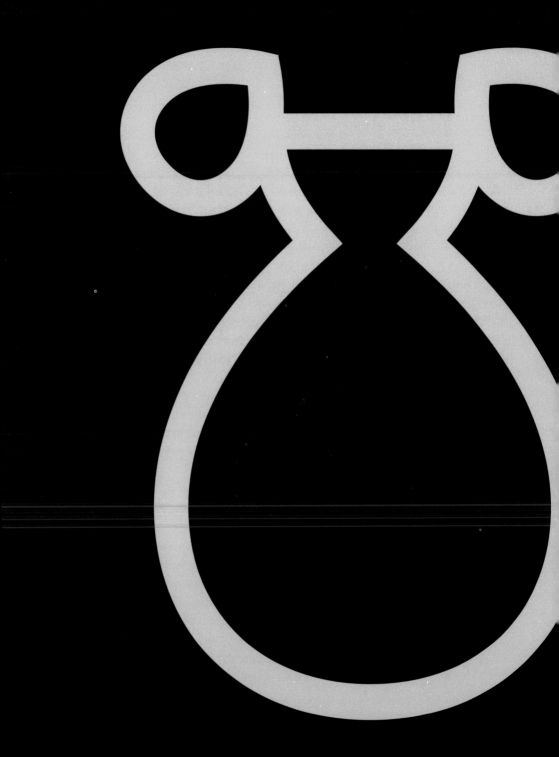

what are you

wearing?

Bridesmaids' attire

It's usual for the bride to choose the bridesmaids' outfits. Traditionally, these were paid for by the bridesmaids themselves for the privilege of taking part. Nowadays, payment is either shared or negotiated – but it's a good idea to discuss this up front. Once you add up the cost of the material, shoes, dressmaking and accessories, it can turn out to be an expensive business.

Choosing the dresses

The bride's choice of bridesmaids' dresses will depend on several factors, most importantly what she is wearing herself. If she chooses a long elaborate gown, then her bridesmaids can be similarly attired. If, however, she decides to marry in a shorter, simpler style, then it would look odd for the attendants to be all frills and flounces.

If the bridesmaids are of varying shapes and sizes, choosing a style and colour to suit them all can be tricky if not impossible. One solution is for the bride to choose material of a certain shade and for the bridesmaids to have dresses made in that same shade but in a style that suits them. Once the style and fabric have been chosen, the chief bridesmaid should coordinate the other bridesmaids' fitting sessions, to take the pressure off the bride. Making the bridesmaids' dresses is a much more popular option than making the bride's dress because they are often simpler in design and decoration, and they can be made at home more easily. Do you know anyone in the close family circle who would be happy to take on the dressmaking task? Saving

money on this aspect means that the bride will be able to splurge a bit more on the fabric and all the accessories.

Some brides and bridesmaids visit high-street stores en masse and choose various off-the-peg dresses that work together and suit each bridesmaid. This can be a much cheaper option too.

Accessories

Bridesmaids often, but not always, wear headdresses and usually carry flowers. Colour and style are important here, as a certain style of headdress may not suit all age groups and individual face shapes and colourings. You may want to research some options here to present to the bride so that she has an idea of the range to choose from.

Shoes are generally formal, matching coloured or light court shoes or sandals for the adults, with soft shoes, such as ballet pumps, for the young ones.

And the children?

The job of these junior helpers is chiefly to take part in the bridal procession to and from the marriage venue, looking as sweet and endearing as possible.

Flower girls generally wear a mini version of either the bride's dress or the bridesmaids' dresses. Usually, they carry a posy or a basket of flowers or petals, which they strew up the aisle in front of the bride. However, some ministers don't appreciate this, so get permission first.

Page-boys are often dressed in sailor suits or Little Lord Fauntleroy outfits. Usually, you can get only a very young boy to agree to this kind of outfit without a fight, so some flexibility is called for. Alternatives are smart trousers and waistcoats, or even a slightly less overwhelming kind of morning dress (if that's what the ushers are wearing). They do not carry flowers.

Who's paying?

Who shells out for the bridesmaids' dresses is a matter of some debate. Traditionally, bridesmaids were provided with material from which to make a dress to their own design. The bride could dictate only the colour, the rest was down to them to make whatever suited best.

Modern brides are keen to be more coordinated and most want to have some control over the bridesmaids' outfits. In these cases, then, the bride or her family should pay. However, parents do sometimes pay for their children's clothes and older bridesmaids might help out with the cost of their dresses, especially if they know that the budget is tight.

If the bride is letting you choose what you wear, and it's something you can wear again, you also might want to contribute to the cost. Alternatively, you might pay towards your shoes, handbag or jewellery. If a lot of money is being spent, it's wise to get something that can be worn again, to a ball or a smart dinner. Another option is for the bride to sell the outfits on afterwards, so consider this as an option.

When it comes to money, just make sure that everything is clear. If a friend asks you to be bridesmaid, it's perfectly acceptable to ask fairly early on whether you will have to fork out for your outfit. If she is choosing an expensive designer number for you and would like you to pay for it yourself, it might affect your decision on whether or not to be a bridesmaid.

Remember to schedule time in your diary for proper dress fittings if you're having something made to measure. If you're chief bridesmaid, you should coordinate the other bridesmaids' fitting sessions, to take the pressure off the bride. All the bridesmaids should meet up at least once before the wedding day, and the chief bridesmaid can organize this.

For more tips and ideas on accessories and what to wear, visit the Fashion and Beauty section on our website (www.confetti.co.uk).

Dressed to the nines
Below is a list of all the items the bride *could* be wearing on the big day. It provides a useful guide for ways in which the bridesmaids' outfits can complement that of the bride. Say you all wear the same tiara, for example.
- Tiara or hat
- Dress/two-piece suit
- Jacket or shawl
- Choker/pendant
- Charm bracelet
- Brooch or earrings
- Belt/sash
- Tights or stockings
- Shoes
- Bag/purse
- Bouquet/posy

Have your say

Most of us are honoured to be asked to be a bridesmaid for a friend or relative, but however close you are to the bride it's not always plain sailing, especially when it comes to choosing what you will wear.

While there are no hard-and-fast rules about bridesmaids' outfits, the bottom line is that it is the bride's day and it is likely that she will have some pretty clear ideas about what she wants. So, how do you keep her happy and still get your point across?

Get involved

If you are worried that the bride might dress you like a meringue or a shepherdess, get involved in the process from the outset. This doesn't mean forcing your ideas on her, but why not suggest a girls' night in with some wine and wedding magazines, and gently let her know what delights (and horrifies) you?

If there are to be several of you, arrange a shopping day soon after the wedding day is announced (with the bride of course!) and try on a wide range of outfits. It will soon become clear what does and doesn't work for you all. If one bridesmaid lives a long way away, email or SMS her pictures of different styles and get her opinion.

If none of the bridesmaids live near enough one another for a practical shopping day, then you could suggest to the bride that she provides the material and you have dresses made in the same fabric, but different styles – which is actually the way bridesmaids' outfits were traditionally made.

Be constructive

Think carefully about any objections before voicing them to the bride, and consider whether they are actually valid. For example, a life-long aversion to peach taffeta is really not a good enough reason to upset the bride. On the other hand, if you are allergic to a certain fabric it's reasonable that you avoid an outfit that is going to cause you discomfort.

Equally, just because you live in trainers, it doesn't mean you should complain at having to sport heels for the day. However, if you really hate your legs but the bride wants you in a mini skirt, then it's definitely worth trying to reach some sort of compromise.

Typical pitfalls

A chief bridesmaid is best armed with a bit of knowledge on potential problems on the dress front, to alert the bride and have a solution to hand to allay her worry and fears.

All shapes and sizes

Bridesmaids come in all shapes and sizes, with different hair colours and skin tones. So, it's rare that you can apply a 'one style and one colour for all' approach when choosing dresses. A good practical solution can be to opt for the same style and type of fabric but each in a different colour. This can look really stunning. Choosing a black-tie dress code is another way to solve the bridesmaid issue.

If there are a number of bridesmaids, it's difficult to get everyone together for shopping trips. So do as much advance research with the bride as you possibly can to minimize the organization involved. Bridesmaids' outfits can usually be found in all the same outlets as bridal wear.

Picking out the best

The bride might choose the chief bridesmaid, officially known as a matron of honour if she is married, to stand out in a different colour or style of dress. Alternatively, the bride could base the outfit on the other bridesmaids but add something extra, say a wrap or some gloves.

If the bride has chosen you as best woman rather than a bridesmaid, then she may want to select a smart suit (skirt or trousers) and hat outfit. To ensure people realize that you are part of the wedding party, try to ensure that the outfit ties in with the wedding's colour theme.

One of the bridesmaids is pregnant

One of the subjects on which Aunt Betti, confetti's agony aunt, receives most mail from panicking brides is the problem of the bridesmaid who announces she is pregnant. Although this is a tricky situation, as no one can know with any certainty what size the bridesmaid will be on the day, it is by no means insurmountable. As well as checking the advice for pregnant brides, consider these options:

• Buy the bridesmaids' outfits from department stores and retailers with large stock lines and a wide range of sizes. This way you can leave it to the last possible moment to find the right size – and you don't have to wait for delivery.

• Have the bridesmaids' outfits made by a seamstress – this way the pregnant bridesmaid can have her dress made last.

What should the flower girls wear?

The littlest bridesmaids, often known as flower girls, carry a small bouquet or basket of either flowers or petals to sprinkle as they walk down the aisle. They may wear a different outfit from the other bridesmaids: some brides like to dress them in little flower fairy costumes, which is sure to be a hit with the girls themselves. A new trend in the US is for the flower girl to dress as a mini-bride in white and a veil.

Whatever outfit the bride chooses, bear in mind that kids grow at an alarming rate. Don't buy the outfit too far in advance, or you'll be looking for another child to fit into it!

Flower girl accessories depend upon the dress, but may include a veil, a wreath of flowers or decorative hairclips.

Whose wedding is it after all?

It's easy to get carried away at the best of times when helping to plan and organize a wedding but as a bridesmaid you have to rein back and remind yourself that the big day is not your big day but the bride's. So, diplomacy and sacrifice are the order of the day.

Something to suit everyone

Choosing outfits to suit all the bridesmaids can be tricky if there are lots of them or they span a large age range. Adults won't want to be dressed the same as children, and hopefully your bride will also bear in mind that the outfit(s) she picks need to flatter people of different ages (and sizes); if she doesn't, you have the option of dropping a few helpful hints.

It's just one day...

While being a bridesmaid is a big deal, it is after all just one day. Before you risk falling out with the bride over her choice of outfit, you should ask yourself whether it is really worth upsetting her. Hear what some bridesmaids said of their dresses:

'My friend Francesca chose the bridesmaids' dresses by herself when she got married – and they were horrible,' recalls Caroline, who still shudders at the memory of her bridesmaid's outfit.

'My dress was a vile shade of green and accentuated all my bad points, as well as not fitting me properly. It looked ridiculous – in fact, my family still laugh at the photos of me in it. But to this day, I've never told Francesca I didn't like it.

She thought the bridesmaids' outfits were lovely, so I just decided to grin and bear it.'

Put up or shut up

Let's face it, most brides want everybody to be happy on their special day, so it is unlikely that she will want you to wear something completely hideous. However, if you feel there is likely to be a clash then maybe you should think very carefully before you agree to be a bridesmaid in the first place.

On the other hand, if you think she is deliberately trying to make you look ridiculous, maybe she's not quite the friend you thought she was...

Safety in numbers

If you are really unhappy with what is proposed, try talking to the other bridesmaids to get their view. If they are all happy, then you will probably have to grin and bear it. If not, then try to find a gentle way to talk to the bride, but make sure that she doesn't feel as if you are ganging up on her. Problems can arise if one bridesmaid is being difficult about her dress. It's then up to the others to find out what the problem is and be diplomatic to get things back on track.

'All of us were fine about the dresses Claire wanted us to wear, but one bridesmaid, Jessica, really kicked up a fuss,' Laura remembers. 'It turned out that she was very self-conscious about her arms and really didn't want to wear something sleeveless. Once the bride knew what the problem was, she managed to find a little jacket that went with the outfit and everything was fine. A lot depends on the bride being flexible in this sort of situation, though.'

A traditional affair

A traditional wedding usually sees the bride wearing white, although very pale pinks, blues, greens and creams are gaining popularity. The dress is usually quite a formal affair, fitted at the bust and waist, with a long, shaped or flowing, sometimes multi-layered skirt (hence the nickname 'meringue'). For the groom, the most common attire for a traditional wedding is the morning suit, with black tie running a close second. Generally, the other members of the wedding party – that's you (as a bridesmaid), the best man, ushers and parents of the bride and groom, are expected to follow suit.

Traditional bridesmaids' attire is usually a dress in a similar style to that of the bride – albeit less elaborate in design – and in a complementary or contrasting colour. Popular styles include the strapless, full-length ball gown, the empire-line dress (which has a seam just below the bust) and the 'princess' style dress, with fitted bust and flared skirt. It used to be that all bridesmaids wore the same design of dress in the same colour, regardless of shape, height and skin type. This can often be a cause for concern, as bridesmaids come in all shapes and sizes. A more favourable approach is for the girls in the wedding party to have different style dresses in the same fabric, or an identical dress in different tones of the same colour.

Accessories for a traditional wedding can include a veil or tiara for the bride, with matching tiaras for the bridesmaids, gloves and little bags or purses. It is also likely that the bridesmaids will wear the same shoes as each other (or at least shoes of the same colour) and will have bouquets to match that of the bride.

The bridal gown shop

This shop is like no other you'll probably go in. The bridal gown shop can be an extremely daunting place. Luckily for you, the bride has to negotiate the many different designs and the somewhat intimidating staff before you do. But don't be put off. You will soon become familiar with the place and its people (who will normally be very helpful). After an initial meeting, in which you choose a style of dress (the bride will be involved at this stage, particularly if she is footing the bill) you will be measured up and dressmaking begins. You will need two or three fittings during the process, and it is up to the chief bridesmaid to organize these, so that all girls attend at the same time.

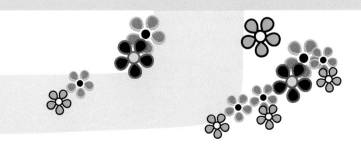

Breaking with convention

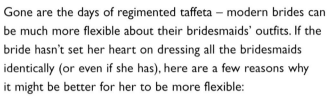

Gone are the days of regimented taffeta – modern brides can be much more flexible about their bridesmaids' outfits. If the bride hasn't set her heart on dressing all the bridesmaids identically (or even if she has), here are a few reasons why it might be better for her to be more flexible:

- The bridesmaids have different heights and figures.
- There is a mix of child and adult attendants.
- The bridesmaids are from different cultural backgrounds.

There are several ways to create a unifying look, while retaining individuality and flexibility.

Choose the same colour

It's perfectly acceptable to select a favourite colour and ask the bridesmaids to choose something in that shade. In the US, black or black and white for bridesmaids is a popular option and creates a very sophisticated look for the big day.

Material matters

A popular option is for the bride to choose a fabric and let the bridesmaids get their dresses made from the same material. That way they will be able to choose a style that suits them and still retain the bridesmaid's look.

The long and short of it

If the bridesmaids are going to choose different dresses it can look a little odd if some are in full length silk and others in short mini dresses. By agreeing on a length you will create a certain uniformity.

Separates solutions

Separates are becoming increasingly popular among modern bridesmaids. Choosing two-piece styles gives a wider scope of tops in the same colour and fabric. It also enables a matron of honour or chief bridesmaid to stand out from the other attendants by having a differently styled top.

Same dress, different colours

This can create a really effective look, especially if your bridesmaids have very different colourings and complexions. You may be limited by the choice of colours in high-street shops, but most wedding outlets have a wide range of swatches for their bridesmaids' ranges and so you should be able to find the colours you are after.

Adults only

No adult really wants to appear at a wedding dressed the same as a toddler. Children in identical dresses can look adorable, but if there are to be adult attendants too, it is usually best to contrast their outfits with those of the children rather than match them.

Dress shapes

When it comes to choosing a style, whether it's for the bride or for the bridesmaids, there are a few rules to follow to find the perfect dress and to make sure you all look beautiful. Knowing that you're wearing a style that suits your body shape will make a huge difference to how you look, and it will also boost your confidence no end.

Here are a few pointers that work for helping the bride choose her dress or choosing the bridesmaids dresses.

- If you are tall and slim you could choose a ballgown with a strapless, fitted bodice.
- If you are thin and feel that your shoulders are rather bony or that your collarbone protrudes too much, go for a long fitted dress, perhaps with a high neckline. You may feel that you are too thin for this style, but your height and leanness could be set off with some delicate detailed embroidery or beading.
- If you are short with a fuller, feminine figure, try an empire line dress. The beauty of this style is that it has a seam under the bust and, in the right fabric, the dress will not cling to your body but flow around it. Although a knee-length dress could also look good, this longer shape will give you a taller silhouette. If you choose to have sleeves, go for long and narrow but not too tight.
- If you have a very full bust, divert attention from it by having a long bodice. Dresses that use the natural waistline, on the other hand, will draw attention to the bust area. Make sure

your bodice area is very plain, and avoid low necklines. If you are really keen on detail, save it for the hem of the skirt.

- If you have full or wide hips then avoid a bustle, peplum or anything tiered. Most styles of dress will look great, but make sure you choose something that doesn't fit too tightly over the hip area. The 'princess' style, which is fitted on top and then flares slightly to the hem, will disguise larger hips. Even the ballgown look, in quite a simple material, will draw attention away from the hips.
- If you have wide shoulders consider narrowing your look with wide straps, or cover your shoulders completely and draw the focus to a V-neckline. It's important to show some skin around this area, but you can soften the effect by wearing a sheer wrap around your shoulders. Stay away from puffed sleeves.
- If your legs are short or on the heavy side it's a good idea to opt for a long dress. Give yourself more height with a sheath style, which is straight, but not too body-hugging.
- If your arms are on the short side then three-quarter-length sleeves will help to make them look longer, but, whatever you do, do not go sleeveless.
- If your arms are chubby go for long and simple sleeves that aren't skin tight.

The right underwear

Just as the bride is kitting herself out with some new lingerie, you and the other bridesmaids need to consider what to wear underneath your outfits. Wearing the wrong size or wrong style bra isn't just uncomfortable – it can make you look lumpy in all the wrong places. Here's how to make sure that doesn't happen to you.

Always get fitted

The style of bra you choose will depend on the cut of your dress. As soon as you've decided on the dress, buy the bra you're going to wear in time for your first fitting, so that your dress can be measured around your underwear. If you're getting a dress 'off the peg', then buy your underwear before you set out on the shopping trip for your outfit.

The right size bra will give you support, a flattering shape and a proper fit to your dress. But many women make the mistake of buying bras that are too big around the rib cage or too small in the cup, which can create 'four-breast syndrome' – breasts spilling over the cup – and ruin your look. What's more, bras can differ in fit and size according to the make and brand. So it's not safe to assume the size you are in one brand will hold true for another.

Bra fittings are free and available in the lingerie department of most department stores or specialist lingerie shops. Take your time during your fitting, until you're satisfied that your fitter has found you a bra that feels comfortable; in fact, you shouldn't be able to feel it at all.

Safe and secure

What you wear underneath your dress plays a vital role in making you feel and look your best. The last thing you want to be worrying about is whether everything is staying in place. Once you've tried on a bra, don't just stand still in it. Walk around; raise your arms and so on. It's important to see if it's still comfortable when you're moving about, as this is what you'll be doing as you meet and greet guests.

What style should I buy?

There's a vast array of styles available from minimizer to push-up. Your bra provides the foundation to your dress, so consider which bra is appropriate for what you're planning to wear. If you've chosen a strapless dress, you'll need a strapless bra or basque; the latter is great for creating a smooth line under dresses and, because they're boned, you can wear them without straps and still feel supported.

Stick to smooth bras for wearing underneath fitted or sheer tops. And to ensure your bra is invisible under white or pale-coloured tops, a nude colour is much better than a white one.

Frills and spills

It is tempting to splurge on fancy underwear for this special occasion, and that is all very well, but make sure it is comfortable. You are going to be wearing it for a long day and need it to offer flexibility as well as comfort if you intend to get on the dance floor. If stockings and suspenders are not your thing, do not torture yourself by wearing them. Do go for feminine frills and laces if they make you feel good, but avoid colours, patterns and textures that may show through your dress or interfere with the line of the gown.

The right shoes

Finding a pair of shoes to complement your dress should be fun, not stressful, as long as you go about it the right way. Here's how to find the ideal pair and how to wear them like a pro...

Finding the perfect shoe

Once you've got your dress, start looking for your shoes straight away. Think fancy shoes for a simple dress or pair simple shoes with an elaborate gown; this rule of thumb can take some of the confusion out of finding the right shoe. And always buy the right size.

It's also a good idea to go shoe shopping in the afternoon. Your feet change shape during the day, depending what you've been getting up to, and they can be a bit puffier in the afternoon. So to choose the right size, try them on in the morning and the afternoon before buying them.

Practise, practise, practise
Don't forget the comfort factor. You're going to be on your feet for hours and the last thing you'll want at the end of the day is aching, blistered feet. Be sure to break in your shoes for an hour a day starting at least a week before the big do. If you chose super-high heels, practise walking in them wearing your dress to avoid a nightmarish trip as you approach the church steps or the dance floor.

Which fabrics are best?

You'll want to match your shoes to the fabric at the hem of
your gown, rather than the bodice. When choosing your shoes
take a swatch of the fabric from your dress.

When should I buy my shoes?

You should have bought your shoes by the time your gown
is ready for any alterations, as you'll need to take them along
to every fitting to ensure the hemline remains the same.

How high is too high?

When it comes to heels, go only as high as feels
comfortable. Heels are great because they add length
to your silhouette. Opt for the same height you wear
day to day. If you're a slave to your trainers, but want
to wear a heel, start wearing heels a bit more regularly
beforehand (wedges and platforms don't count) to get
your feet and body used to the idea. Alternatively,
compromise – wear a low kitten heel.

**How can I keep my
feet dancing?**
Sprinkle talc into shoes
to absorb moisture –
when your feet sweat
and swell, your shoes
are more likely to rub.
Add specially designed
gel padding under the
ball of each foot.

The right hat

A special occasion provides the perfect excuse to wear a hat or headpiece, but how do you get it right? If you've decided to wear a hat to top off your bridesmaid's finery, we will steer you safely through the maze of the millinery department. The hat you choose has to work quite hard: it must be the right shape for your face, your body type, your outfit and your hairstyle; and not steal the limelight from the bride. This can feel like a tall order but it is achievable. Here's how.

Take your time

When hat shopping, allow yourself a good hour for trying on different styles. As you get used to seeing yourself in a hat the easier it will be to work out which styles suit you best. Take a friend for an extra opinion, too.

Team it up right

Always choose your hat to match your outfit and not the other way around. A hat should complement your outfit, not overpower it. If your outfit is fairly dressy, then opt for a simple hat – and vice versa.

Your hat or headpiece should complement your entire outfit. Do remember, however, to match your shoes with your handbag and not your hat – when your hat comes off, your shoes may otherwise look lost on your outfit. As a rule, think, light straw fabrics for spring/summer; felts and fabrics should be kept for autumn/winter.

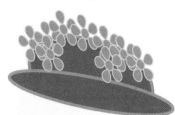

Get the shape right

Never buy a hat simply because it's the right colour. What you're looking for is a hat shape to complement the shape of your face.

Tall crowned hats suit round faces, while snugger styles provide a frame for longer faces. Rounded crowns suit just about every face, while square crowns work for larger heads. As a rule the crown of your hat should never be narrower than your cheekbones.

Women with wide-set eyes can wear almost any hat, but others look best in a hat with brim worn low to the brow.

Match your personality

When choosing a hat, don't forget to factor in your personality. If you allow your hat to be an expression of who you are then you may be able to get away with breaking all the rules.

Finding the right fit

As with gloves and shoes, the right hat is all about fit. When trying on a hat, position it in the centre of your head so that it is covering up half of your forehead. An all-to-common mistake is to sit your hat too far back on the crown of your head or perch it on the top of your head. Pull it down low and wear it with confidence. And don't be shy to walk around the shop wearing it to get a sense of how it feels.

A hat to enhance your look

Want to add inches to your height without wearing heels? If you're small you can use a hat to give the impression of extra height. A headpiece with a bit of height can also make you look taller. And simply wearing a hat that matches the colour of the top part of your outfit can give the illusion of a longer profile.

Do bear in mind that, generally speaking, large hats tend to swamp petite frames and smaller hats are lost on women with larger frames.

Finishing touches

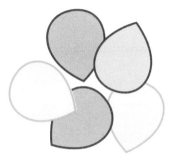

The gloves are off

If you're wearing a strapless, sleeveless or thin-strapped dress, gloves that extend over your elbow (opera length) make an elegant accent. Short or cap-sleeve dresses look great with gloves that come just to your elbow, while wrist-length gloves make a perfect choice for all lengths of sleeve.

Bag it up

Whether you need a ready supply of make-up or tissues, or somewhere to stash your keepsakes, a handbag of some sort is pretty much essential. The style of bag you choose depends on your outfit. But if you follow the rule of opposites and pair a simple bag with a dramatic dress and an ornate bag with a simple frock, then you can't go too far wrong.

All that glitters...

When it comes to jewellery, less is definitely more. Think simple and understated. When choosing jewellery, your dress should always be the starting point. If your dress sparkles with crystals, pick jewellery with matching accents. The colour is important, too. Jewellery can give your outfit

a real wow factor. So use it to accentuate your best features: eyes, cheekbones, décolletage, neck and hair. If you're wearing your hair up, for instance, drop earrings give a dramatic touch. For short hair, studs are a great choice. If you've decided to leave your long hair loose teamed with a pair of chandelier earrings, don't overwhelm the effect by adding a necklace as well.

Theme it

Is the event a themed one? Your choice of accessories is an easy way to refer to the theme without having to buy a dress that you may only be able to wear once. A gold wedding anniversary party, say, doesn't necessarily require a completely gold outfit – but a glamorous pair of gold shoes or stunning gold earrings will do the trick. So, think laterally too.

Keep it simple

If you've decided to wear a headpiece, opt for something with classic, clean lines. An ornate dress is best combined with an understated headpiece, while a simple, classically cut dress makes a great foil for a more flamboyant headpiece and dramatic pieces such as a jewelled tiara.

Looking beautiful

Getting into shape

You want your body to be at its best on the wedding day, but the solution isn't to starve yourself. With a healthy diet, exercise and a little bit of professional help, you'll be a truly radiant bridesmaid.

You may have decided to lose a few pounds before the wedding day, but don't set yourself unrealistic targets. It's never easy to stick to a diet, and when you're feeling stressed, it's even harder. If the bride is trying to shed a few pounds, too, then try to give each other moral support, and stick to the plan even on those shopping-day lunches.

Effective dieting isn't about calorie counting, it's about changing your eating habits. So tuck into more high-carbohydrate foods (cereals, bread, rice, pasta, potatoes) and fewer high-fat foods (cheese, ice cream, red meat, fried breakfasts). Get into the habit of eating like this all the time and aim to lose 0.5–1 kg (1–2 lb) a week.

Try to take some extra exercise, such as walking to work or swimming. This should burn off a few pounds but, more importantly, it will make you feel healthier and more relaxed.

If you have some spare cash, treat yourself to a day or more at a health spa. Expert advice, beauty therapies and exercise facilities will help you come away feeling fabulous.

Planning your look

Along with the bride, learn the tricks of enhancing your best features. The idea is to look like a better version of yourself rather than going for a completely new look.

Break those old habits and start a regular skincare routine a few months before the wedding. Invest in some good products, and cleanse, tone and moisturize every morning and evening. To find out which products suit your skin, have a makeover in a department store. You'll receive lots of help and advice, and the fee is usually redeemable against any products bought.

Beauty countdown

Follow this beauty countdown to ensure that you will look your best on the bride's big day.

- **12 weeks to go** Facial and shaping of eyebrows to complement the face; waxing; hair cut for wedding style; finish with a relaxing neck and back massage to unwind.
- **10 weeks to go** Manicure and pedicure – strengthening and conditioning nails as well as moisturizing skin on the hands and feet.
- **7 weeks to go** Facial; waxing; neck and back massage.
- **5 weeks to go** Manicure and pedicure – experiment with nail colours.
- **3 weeks to go** Final hair cut and colour, if necessary.
- **1 week to go** Facial (you should now be seeing the results of your regular facials and regular skin routine); waxing; neck and back massage.
- **2 days to go** Trial wedding make-up to establish the look that suits you.
- **1 day to go** Have the final manicure and pedicure, or paint each other's fingernails and toenails and make sure they dry completely.
- **Wedding day** Set aside plenty of time for doing your hair and make-up.

duties on the
big day

Girls together

If circumstances allow, you may want to spend the day or at the very least the evening before the big day with the bride, especially if she's nervous or spending the night apart from the groom. If you're having the day together then you should both have a bridal manicure today.

Now that hen nights are no longer usually held the night before the wedding, it's a great opportunity to have a quiet evening in with some videos and a glass of wine and have a good chat. Encourage her to talk about what she thinks tomorrow will mean to her – the day itself will go so fast it's a good idea to get some of the contemplation in beforehand.

Something old, something new...

The complete phrase is:

Something old, something new
Something borrowed, something blue
And a silver sixpence in her shoe.

Each item represents a token of good luck for the bride. If she carries all of them on her wedding day, her marriage will be a happy one.

- 'Something old' represents the link with the bride's family and the past. The old item is often a piece of family jewellery but can be her mother's or grandmother's wedding dress.
- 'Something new' means optimism and hope for the bride's new life ahead.

- 'Something borrowed' is usually an item from a happily married friend or family member, whose good fortune in marriage is supposed to transfer to the new bride. The borrowed item also reminds the bride that she can depend on her friends and family, and can be an item of jewellery or even a handkerchief, for example.
- 'Something blue' ties in with the fact that blue has had strong connections to weddings for centuries. In ancient Rome, brides wore blue to symbolize love, modesty and fidelity. Christianity has long dressed the Virgin Mary in blue, so purity is traditionally associated with the colour.
- And finally, a silver sixpence in the bride's shoe represents wealth and financial security.

If you like this kind of thing, then check that the bride ticks all the boxes for a happy and prosperous marriage.

Emergency kit

Pack this emergency kit in a bag and ask another guest to leave it in their car to pick up after the ceremony. If the bride loses the back of her earring or a guest breaks a strap on her dress, you'll be able to rush to the rescue.

- Tights
- Tissues
- Baby wipes
- Breath mints
- Safety pins
- Comb/brush
- Lipstick
- Nail file
- Hairgrips
- Hair spray
- Spare earring backs
- Mobile phone (but switched off)
- Pain relief tablets
- Pen

The morning of the wedding

Dressing drill

It makes sense for all the bridesmaids and page-boys to get dressed at the bridal home or wherever the bride is travelling from. This helps to prevent creasing of the wedding outfits and gives everyone the chance to make any last-minute adjustments.

If you're chief bridesmaid, your role on the day is of utmost importance to the bride and the other attendants. You must maintain a calming influence throughout the day and be as organized as possible.

On the morning of the wedding, you'll need to ensure that everyone is where they should be when they should be, that the right clothes and accessories are ready for the right person and that you are prepared to deal with any emergencies that might arise.

Your other duties on the day include: being at the bride's house in plenty of time for the hairdresser and make-up artist; helping to dress the younger attendants, if necessary, and keeping them looking perfect until the transport arrives; looking after emergency supplies – lipstick, tissues, etc. – for the bride throughout the day (see page 85).

The photographer may be at the house during the preparations, depending on his or her brief, so be prepared for candid shots while everyone is getting ready. There may be time for some more organized photos in the garden or getting into and out of the mode of transport.

Before setting off

Most importantly, make sure you organized for your
emergency kit (see page 85) to get to the church (preferably
in the boot of another guest's car) and that the bride has her
bouquet (and any other accessories). Check that all other
attendants are present and correct. If you have very young
attendants to look after – flower girls and page-boys – do
your best to curb any excessive excitement or nervousness.
It may help to be in touch with the best man, to know that
the groom is on his way to the church or venue, if not there
already. Give your bride a final hug or squeeze of the hand
and wish her parents well.

Getting there

It is usual for the chief bridesmaid, bridesmaids and other
attendants to travel to the ceremony venue with the bride's
mother. Your calming influence may now be tested to the
limit, as everyone will be excited and perhaps a little
emotional about the forthcoming events.

Once all the attendants are assembled, the photographer
may want to take some pictures outside the venue before
the bride arrives. The chief bridesmaid will have to organize
the other bridesmaids and page-boys, particularly any very
young ones.

The wedding ceremony

Church wedding

If the ceremony is in a church, you will need to:

- Meet the bride at the church door and organize any other attendants of the bride.
- Arrange the bride's veil and train before she proceeds down the aisle.

After the marriage service, you will accompany the best man along with the bride and groom to the vestry for the signing of the register. You may also be asked by the bride to sign the register as a witness. Once all the formalities are over, the best man will escort you down the aisle as part of the recessional, following in line after the bride and groom, the bride's father and groom's mother and the groom's father and bride's mother.

Register office or other venue wedding

Your role at the register office is very similar to that in a church. As the form of the service can vary according to what the bride and groom would like, check with the bride beforehand about where she would like you to be: walking behind her on the way in or waiting at the front if she chooses to walk in with her groom. As at the church, you may be required to be one of the two witnesses who sign the register with the bride and groom at the end of the wedding ceremony.

Duties at the ceremony

It's a good idea to know by heart what you're going to be doing during the service; you should have been at the rehearsal, which is usually the day before. You follow the bride into the venue (or you may go first, American style) and usually sit near the front. Make sure that you know where to sit (or whether you're to stand during the ceremony) and that any very young attendants have their parents seated close by.

Once the bride has joined the groom, the chief bridesmaid takes her bouquet and gloves, if she is wearing any, and looks after them for the duration of the service. She returns them after the signing of the register.

The chief bridesmaid accompanies the best man as part of the wedding party into the vestry or side room, in a church service, or moves to the side table in a register office for the official signing of the register. Once the recessional music sounds out and the bride and groom make their way down the aisle, the best man escorts the chief bridesmaid immediately following the parents of the bride and groom out of the church or venue. Other older bridesmaids are escorted by the ushers, while younger bridesmaids and page-boys follow behind.

Once everyone is outside, the chief bridesmaid usually works with the best man and photographer to organize the wedding couple and their attendants for some photographs. After the photo session, the next task is to make sure everyone gets to the reception venue. Round up all the younger runaway attendants and bundle them in a car, as necessary, to transport them to the venue.

'Say cheese!'
As a bridesmaid, you can expect to be in a number of the pictures. You can help by sticking with the other attendants at this time, to make sure that the shots run smoothly and promptly. If you are the chief bridesmaid, keep an eye on the child attendants to make sure they are available and behaving appropriately for the photographs. Tradition has it that the chief bridesmaid has her photo taken with the best man.

Duties at the reception

You'll already know from conversations with the bride over the last year whether the wedding is going to be a formal or an informal one. If a certain amount of formality is called for, then ensure you know where you need to be at all times so that you can help the bride and make her day stress-free.

Once at the reception, the bride may want the chief bridesmaid to be a part of the receiving line. The purpose of the line is to allow the guests to meet the bridal party and to ensure that the bride and groom say at least a few words to each guest.

You may have the responsibility for displaying the bride's bouquet somewhere safe (and preferably cool), ensuring it doesn't get damaged during the rest of the day. This is especially important if she is planning to have the flowers preserved as a souvenir.

All the adult bridesmaids should circulate among the guests, ensuring that they are enjoying themselves. But the chief bridesmaid should also check that they are taking advantage of any disposable cameras provided on the tables, so that the bride and groom get to see what everyone else got up to on their big day. In this way you act as the bride's back-up; she will have only limited time to spend with each guest.

Although the speeches at the reception are generally a male prerogative, it is becoming more usual for either bride, chief bridesmaid or even both of you to make a speech. If you're planning on making a speech, turn to Chapters 5, 6 and 7 for top tips and some great ideas (see pages 100–157).

The first dance is exclusively reserved for the newlyweds, but it is traditional for the chief bridesmaid to take to the floor with the best man and join the happy couple midway through the first dance.

Finally, when the couple change into their going-away outfits, the chief bridesmaid should be on hand to take care of the bride's wedding dress and ensure that it is returned to her home or, if necessary, to the hire shop. The other attendants' dresses may need to be returned too.

The thank-yous

No doubt, the bride and groom will present a small gift to all the bridesmaids as a thank you. There is a lovely tradition behind this gift: the giving of extra presents to the bridesmaids is an ancient custom, originating from the days when the groom had to 'catch' his bride and, rather than actually chasing her, he used to bribe her friends to lure her to a place where he could approach her. Visit www.confetti.co.uk/thank-yougifts for ideas.

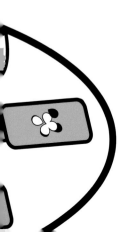

Reception traditions

Depending on the formality of the wedding, there are key elements that make up the reception – from the receiving line and top table to cutting the cake and throwing the bouquet. If the wedding is a traditional one, make sure you know the etiquette and what's required of you for each element.

Speeches and toasts

Most receptions include speeches and toasts. Usually they come at the end of the meal, although there is an increasing trend to have them before the meal begins. Usually, the father of the bride speaks first and then toasts the bride and groom. Next, comes the groom – and perhaps the bride. They thank their guests for coming and, traditionally, the groom proposes a toast to the bridesmaids. Finally, comes the best man, who officially 'replies' on behalf of the bridesmaids. If as chief bridesmaid you'd like to say a few words, your 'spot' is between the bride and the best man.

Favours

It's usual nowadays to give each guest a tiny gift, or favour, to remind them of the wedding day. These range from traditional Italian sugared almonds, more modern confectionery options, such as chocolates or jelly beans, to perfumed candles and even extravagant silver trinkets.

Cutting the cake

The bride and groom cut the cake together as a symbol of their shared future. After the cake-cutting ceremony (usually at the very end of the meal and after the speeches), the caterers remove the cake, which is sliced up and handed round to guests.

The first dance

Traditionally, the bride and groom have the 'first dance' together. This would have been a waltz in the past, but nowadays it's whatever they choose. If they don't relish the idea of dancing in public, they may well open the dance floor to everyone as soon as the music starts.

Traditionally, the best man joins in midway through the first dance with the chief bridesmaid, while the ushers dance with the other bridesmaids. It is also traditional for the groom to dance with his new mother-in-law and then with his mother, while the bride dances with her new father-in-law and then her father.

Timely departure

Guests are supposed to remain at the reception until the couple leave, so if there is to be no formal 'going away', let your guests know (especially the older ones) that you intend to dance the night away!

Tossing the bouquet

After the reception, the bride throws her bouquet over her shoulder towards a group of her unmarried girlfriends and female relatives. Traditionally, the one who catches the flowers (and survives the scrum!) will be the next to marry.

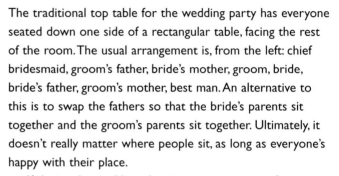

The top table

The traditional top table for the wedding party has everyone seated down one side of a rectangular table, facing the rest of the room. The usual arrangement is, from the left: chief bridesmaid, groom's father, bride's mother, groom, bride, bride's father, groom's mother, best man. An alternative to this is to swap the fathers so that the bride's parents sit together and the groom's parents sit together. Ultimately, it doesn't really matter where people sit, as long as everyone's happy with their place.

If during the wedding planning you are aware of any resentment or bitterness lurking between particular people, for example, current partners and exes, prompt the bride to bear this in mind during the table planning. If there is a large extended family, the bride might need to be a little more creative with the 'top table' arrangement. A round (non-hierarchical) table is always a good way to solve this problem.

While it's best to avoid seating sworn enemies next to each other, sometimes it's unavoidable. If this happens, warn

each person in advance and trust that their love for the bride and/or groom will take precedence over their mutual animosity. It's important to remember that the onus is on others to cooperate and be at least civil to one another. It's not for the happy couple to come up with the seating plan from heaven that will magically wipe out all tension.

Stay focused

While it's easy to get completely absorbed in the speech you might be making after the meal, try to remind yourself what your priorities are and that your role is a multiple one. The bride is number one priority, with the other bridesmaids coming second, closely followed by the rest of the guests. Organizing the bridesmaids, introducing guests to one another and generally making sure everything runs smoothly are all part of your job, and it's a good idea to work closely with the best man for a successful event. If you concentrate on doing these things, you'll not only be fulfilling your role properly, but you'll also be distracting yourself from any pre-speech nerves.

Party time!

Once the speeches are out of the way you can relax a little. It's tradition for the best man to dance with the chief bridesmaid first, joining the bride and groom midway through the first dance or perhaps for the second dance.

Even though you can let your hair down a little, your responsibilities are not over yet. You need to keep a general eye on the proceedings. If wedding cameras have been put out on the guests' tables, for example, ensure they are used throughout the reception. If the best man has ideas about decorating the bride and groom's car – or whatever transport is taking them away from the venue that evening – make sure that while it's fun it doesn't amount to criminal damage. The happy – and hapless – couple will be relying on it, so bear in mind that the car needs to remain in working order, especially if they are going straight off on their honeymoon and need to catch trains or flights later.

Or perhaps some or all of the bridesmaids arrange a secret liaison with the hotel manager (if the wedding couple are staying at the venue) to get access to the bridal suite to give the newlyweds a surprise – a nice one! Scatter rose petals or confetti over the bed (and in between the sheets) and arrange for a bottle of bubbly to be chilled and waiting for them when they turn in.

Finally, when the time comes, assist the hosts in bringing the celebrations to a close, making sure everyone has transport home or can find their room if they are staying overnight at the reception venue. The hosts – especially if they are the bride and groom – may appreciate it if you offer to check the bill and ensure any outstanding payments are settled for them at the end of the night.

With your partner in crime (aka the best man), take a last look round the venue before you leave for any stray presents or lost property. Collect them together and keep them safe until you can return them to their rightful owners. As soon as possible after the wedding, arrange to collect any hired outfits so that they can be returned and deposits refunded.

Checklist of duties on the day

- If you have been in charge of the flowers, phone to check they have arrived at the correct venues and make sure the supplier has been paid.
- If you have organized the wedding cake, phone to check that it has been delivered to the venue and assembled, as necessary.
- If you or any of the other bridesmaids are giving a reading, make sure you/they have the text to hand.
- Check that you have your notes with you if you are giving a speech.
- Assist the bride in getting dressed.
- Make sure the other bridesmaids have their bouquets, and that any flower girls and page-boys have petals/confetti if using.
- Round up the attendants 10 minutes before it is time to leave for the ceremony venue, and check they have everything they need in place.
- Greet the bride at the ceremony venue, checking she looks fabulous before entering (no smudged make-up, or crumpled hem lines).
- Coordinate the other attendants at the church or register office, making sure they know what to do and where to sit.
- Help the best man coordinate the photography and encourage the guests to use the disposable cameras; collect those at the end of the reception.
- If the bride is going on honeymoon immediately after the wedding, make sure you have all the right details for anything you have offered to take care of in her absence (see page 99).

After the wedding

For most of the guests at the wedding, once the reception is over, that is that: they have had a great time and can now get on with the rest of their lives. This is unlikely to be the case for you, however. The bride has probably gone off on her honeymoon leaving you with a little list of things to take care of for her. And, depending on how keen you were to help out with the arrangements for her wedding, this list could be quite long.

- If you have had any involvement with arranging flowers or the wedding cake, there may be a balance of payment to be made, or equipment that needs returning (vases, platters, for example). By the way, it is a nice gesture to clean anything before taking it back.

- You may have been allocated the task of sending cake to absent guests – an old custom that is often upheld at traditional weddings. If so, you will need names and addresses before the bride leaves for her honeymoon; or liaise with the bride's and the groom's families for contact details.

- The bride may have made you responsible for getting flowers from the wedding to various female friends and relatives. This should happen the day after the do (or the day after that at the very latest), if you want to avoid turning up with a wilting mess.

- If you and the other bridesmaids hired your dresses for the wedding, you will definitely be responsible for getting them back to the supplier in good time.

- It is not unusual for the chief bridesmaid and best man to make sure that any wedding gifts reach the couple's home safely in their absence. If this is the case, you will need to liaise with the best man, and the reception venue, to arrange a good time for this.

Etiquette corner
Finally, though not obligatory, a letter to each set of parents might be in order, congratulating them on the marriage of their son/daughter, and thanking them for their generosity if they have been involved in the proceedings. This is particularly welcome if you have known the bride (and groom) for a long time.

making a
speech

The chief bridesmaid's speech

It's still a relatively new idea for the chief bridesmaid – or best woman – to make a speech, but if the bride plans to speak it can be a nice touch if you do, too. Your speech is pretty much a free zone, tradition-wise. You'll probably want to talk about your relationship with the bride, about her and the groom, perhaps adding some stories from the hen night or the wedding build-up.

Obviously the formality of your speech depends on the formality of the occasion, but if you are the bride's sister, or your relationship with her as a very old friend is well known, then you can get away with poking a bit more fun at her! As chief bridesmaid or maid/matron of honour, you have fewer compulsory elements to include in your speech and the greater part of it can be about the bride, your relationship with her and her relationship with the groom.

What to include

Make sure that in your speech, you:
- Compliment the bride and thank her for choosing you as her chief bridesmaid.
- Comment on the preparations for the wedding – this is the time you have spent together, both in the run-up to the day and in the time directly before the ceremony.
- Share a memory of the bride that highlights an amusing or endearing part of her personality.
- Compliment the ushers on behalf of the bridesmaids.
- Toast the bride and groom.

Who speaks and when...

The formal order of speakers is:

- Father of the bride (or a close family friend)
- The groom
- The bride (if she'd like to speak)
- The chief bridesmaid (if she'd like to speak)
- The best man

Traditionally, the speeches take place after the meal, but some couples decide to have them beforehand to allow the speakers to enjoy their meal free of nerves.

...And who says what?

As with your speech, particular thank-yous and acknowledgements are expected in each person's speech.

Father of the bride
(or the person giving the bride away)
- Thanks the guests for coming.
- Thanks everyone who has contributed to the cost of the wedding.
- Compliments the bride, and welcomes her new husband into the family.
- Toasts the bride and groom.

Bridegroom
- Thanks the father of the bride for his toast.
- Thanks the guests for attending and for their gifts.
- Thanks both sets of parents.
- Compliments his bride.
- Thanks his best man.
- Thanks and toasts the bridesmaids.

Bride
- Reiterates the thanks already given – especially for the gifts.
- Thanks anyone who has not already been thanked by the speakers or may not be mentioned by them.
- Compliments her groom.

Best man
- Thanks the groom for his toast to the bridesmaids.
- Comments on the bridal couple, particularly the groom.
- Reads out any messages from absent friends and relatives.
- Toasts the bride and groom.

Cardinal rules

Unaccustomed as you are, you may well be scheduled for a spot of speech-making, depending on what you've arranged with the bride and groom. Stick to the cardinal rules and you will make your piece a sure-fire success.

Pick the right tone

Tone can be tricky, as you have to fulfil certain obligations.

- You need to express thanks and convey affection and sincerity. You want to avoid coming across as too serious, dull or even pompous.
- The ideal tone is one of gentle humour, intimacy and affection. Try to aim for something that makes everyone feel included.

Keep it short

However fabulous your speech, the golden rule is to leave your audience wanting more.

- Wedding guests enjoy speeches, but don't overestimate their boredom threshold. With speeches, less is always more and brevity really is the soul of wit.
- Stick to quick-fire quips rather than shaggy-dog stories; anecdotes rather than sagas; pithy comments rather than rambling digressions.
- To help you get it right, time yourself when you practise.

Don't wing it

Take time to prepare and write your speech.

- Make a start on your speech a few weeks before the wedding and jot down ideas as they occur to you.
- Ask others for anecdotes, and use books and quotations.
- Rehearse your performance, preferably in front of people you can rely on for honest, constructive feedback.

The cardinal sins
Wedding speeches should be memorable. But make sure guests remember your speech for the right reasons. Here's what *not* to do.

Don't mention the war...

Aim to make your speech appeal to everyone and, most importantly, avoid anything that may cause offence.

- If an anecdote can't easily be explained, leave it out.
- Swearing is a definite no-go area. The last thing you need is a granny fainting at a four-letter word.
- And, whatever feelings you may have about the couple's compatibility, this is not the time to let your hostility show.

Don't ramble

Being asked to speak at a wedding is a compliment, so plan what you are going to say properly.

- Create a definite structure with a beginning, middle and end.
- Keep it short; long, rambling speeches are likely to send the older guests off to sleep.
- Likewise, long drawn-out jokes may fall flat if they take too long.

Don't mumble

Swallowing your words, speaking too fast and losing your place are classic problems.

- As soon as you start your speech, check that everyone in the room can hear you.
- Speak slowly and clearly.

Good preparation

Preparing your speech

Preparation is at the heart of a good speech. Scribbling down a few words the night before the big day is not going to work. You may start formulating some ideas as soon as you decide you are going to give a speech, but keep them on the back burner and really start working on the speech a few weeks before the wedding.

It's an unfailing rule: the more prepared you are, the more confident you will be about giving your speech, and the more your audience will enjoy it. And the more you'll enjoy the experience, too.

Break down each element

Don't think about your speech as one big lump. Break it down into headings and decide what you're going to say under each one. For instance, if you are the best woman or chief bridesmaid – how you met the bride, the wedding preparations, or how the bride and groom got to know each other. Then, look at all the elements and work out the best order in which to fit them together.

Speech-making aids

As you prepare, make sure you have:

- A notebook so you can jot down ideas as they occur to you.
- A tape recorder so you can practise and time your speech.
- Asked friends and family to listen to your speech and give you ideas.
- Decided what props (if any) you are using and how to use them.
- A copy of the latest draft (on the wedding day you may have to ask a friend to carry this as most bridesmaid's outfits don't come with pockets).

What kind of speech to make

Decide what kind of speech you want to make before you start putting it together. You could:

- Make a speech on your own.
- Make a joint speech, perhaps with the best man or another bridesmaid.
- Perform a stunt and/or use props.
- Use a home video or slides or invent funny telegrams.
- Adopt a well-known format to comic effect.

Do your research

Ask friends and family

It sounds obvious, but it's often overlooked – the best way to find out more about the subjects of your speech is to talk to their friends and relatives. Siblings, cousins, old school friends... each will have a different perspective on the stars of the day, and spending time chatting to them is sure to draw out half-forgotten anecdotal gems.

The best way to use this valuable resource is to get a group of friends and family together for a drink and a few reminiscences. While they sit there swapping stories at, say the bridal shower or hen party, you may find the bulk of your speech will have been written for you by the end of the night. Bring along a tape recorder, too, so you can join in without worrying about taking notes.

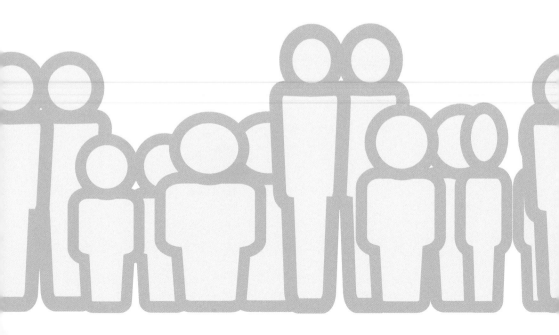

Other sources

Once you've dredged the inner circle,
you could extend your research to other
areas of the past. Look through old photo
albums, letters and cuttings – any of these
might provide something funny to read
out or hold up.

Track down people your subjects
went to school with or worked with, such as former
teachers and bosses. One best woman – the bride's sister –
went through her sister's old school books and found an
essay, written at the age of 11, entitled 'The Man I will Marry'.
Naturally, her reading of this valuable document went down a
treat on the big day.

The right material

Wedding speakers have it tough. Who else has to make a speech that will appeal to an audience with an age range of 2 to 82? Speeches have to make people laugh without offending anyone's sensibilities, talk about families and relationships without treading on anyone's toes and hold people's attention.

Quick speech checklist

- Does your speech fit the occasion? Is it light-hearted and positive?
- Have you tested it on other people and asked for their honest feedback?
- Have you timed it to ensure it's not too long?
- Have you been careful not to offend anyone? Or leave anyone out?
- Do you know in what order the speeches will be made and at what time? (see page 103)
- If there is a microphone, do you know how to use it?
- Have you written notes, in case you dry up?
- Have you checked names and how to pronounce them?
- Have you made a note of everyone you need to thank, or any messages to be read out?

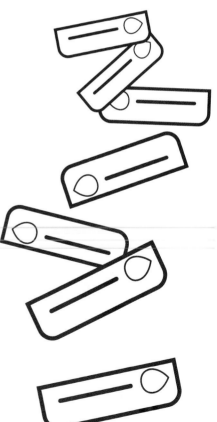

Tailored to fit

The material that you decide is suitable for your speech will depend on your audience. It's up to you to find out who you'll be talking to and to check beforehand that what you want to say won't cause offence. If you can rehearse your speech in front of your mum and granny without them feeling uncomfortable or you feeling embarrassed, you're probably on to a winner.

Tips for success

It sounds like a tall order, but most of the pitfalls of speech-making can be avoided if you know what to talk about and recognize that there are limits around certain subjects. It's all a matter of choosing and using your material with care.

- **Criticism** Weddings aren't the place for criticism. Don't knock anything relating to the venue or the service. Don't make jokes at other people's expense, especially the bride's. This is the happy couple's perfect day, and you need to help keep it that way.
- **The bride** Any ambivalent feelings about the groom should be kept firmly under wraps at the wedding.
- **Be kind** Remember, if you're opting for a funny speech to mix the mockery with some sincerity. Talk about how highly you think of both the bride and the groom, and how their relationship together has enriched each other. Give the couple all your very best wishes for the future.
- **Include everyone** Make sure no one feels left out by considering the different types of people who will be listening to your speech. Avoid in-jokes and make sure you explain references that some listeners may not understand.

Do's and Don'ts

Subject	What's expected	Do Say	Don't Say
The happy couple's relationship	Comments about the bride and groom are usually part of every wedding speech. Tread carefully, however, especially if their relationship has been stormy in the past.	Tell guests about how their first meeting generated enough electricity to power the National Grid. Talk about how compatible they are and how great they both look today.	Don't tell them about how they slept together within half-an-hour of meeting or about how she left him for someone else for six months. Arguments, estrangements and threats to call off the wedding are all off limits. If in any doubt, leave it out.
Girly secret	Guests might be amused to know a girly secret or two – something from your friend's past that she thinks is long forgotten. Something harmless is all part of the fun, but make sure you avoid anything that might cause embarrassment and discomfort.	Tell everyone about the crush she had on Brad Pitt at school, and how she got a detention for scribbling his name on her desk.	She made a pass at the groom's brother while on a double date in the early days of their relationship.
Family matters	Complimenting the bride's and the groom's families can be part of your speech – but make sure you stick to compliments only.	Tell guests how the bride/groom have great parents – and now they're gaining great parents-in-law. Or congratulate the parents for organizing the wedding so well.	Don't tell them how you're amazed to see the bride's father there at all since he walked out when the bride was still in her pram. Speeches shouldn't be used for settling scores.

Subject	What's expected	Do Say	Don't Say
The wedding	Behind-the-scenes stories about preparing for the wedding, especially amusing incidents and narrowly averted disasters, make good ingredients for speeches. However, you might be surprised at how sensitive these subjects can be. Very few families don't have a couple of squabbles over wedding arrangements. These disagreements often seem amusing by the time the big day arrives, but sometimes they don't – so tread carefully.	Tell guests how fantastically the day has turned out and how it's all down to the hard work of all the organizers.	Don't tell them about how the bride's mother almost had a nervous breakdown over the seating plan – unless you're absolutely sure she'll think it's funny. As always, run your speech by someone close to the family first.
In-jokes	Making everyone feel included is an important job of any speaker. You need to explain references that not everyone may be familiar with, and if this takes too long, it's better to think of another anecdote.	Tell guests about how, one year, the bride/groom broke three dozen eggs in the school egg-and-spoon race.	Don't tell them about that time in design and technology class when the bride/groom got told off by Mr Smith, you know, the technology teacher who was really mad... you really had to be there.

A good delivery

It ain't what you do...

As anyone who's made a successful speech will tell you, it's not what you say, it's the way you say it. And, you want to make sure the way you deliver and present your speech does justice to your carefully written masterpiece. Here's how.

Practice makes perfect

Reading your speech out again and again before the big day is essential if you want to perfect your delivery, ensure your material is suitable and find out if your jokes are really funny. Your speech should appeal to everyone, from your friends to the primmest of aunts, so try to rehearse in front of a variety of people.

Test it out on people who will give honest, constructive feedback. They will also be able to tell you when you're mumbling, or rambling, or just going on too long. You should also record your rehearsals on tape. That way, you will be able to review yourself and see where there's room for improvement and how you are for time – aim for five minutes as a rough guide.

The run-up

You've enjoyed a tearful moment during the wedding ceremony and the celebrations and reception have begun. Good food and wine is flowing but all you can think about is how nervous you are about your imminent speech. How you fill your time now will affect your delivery.

Don't overindulge

Although it's very tempting to down a few too many glasses while you're waiting to speak – don't. Being tipsy could affect your delivery by making you slur your words and cause you to be unsteady on your feet. Too many drinks might also lead you to decide that the risqué story that you deleted from your original speech, should really be in there after all.

Have a banana

Many professional performers swear by the trick of eating a banana about 20 minutes before they start speaking. Doing this, they say, will give you a quick energy boost and help steady your nerves.

Ten steps to success

Timing is crucial when it comes to speeches. However brilliant yours is, and however good a speaker you are, five minutes is more than enough. People enjoy listening to speeches, but they also want to get on with talking and dancing, so keep it short. Make sure yours has a firm beginning, middle and end. Steer clear of rambling stories in favour of short, pithy jokes and asides. When it comes to speeches, less is definitely more.

Don't try to begin your speech when there are lots of distractions. Wait until the audience has settled down, stopped applauding the previous speaker and you have people's undivided attention.

1 Make eye contact

When you're making your speech make eye contact – just not with everyone at once. Speak as if you were talking to one person and focus on them. You can look around the room if you want to, but focus on one person at a time. The trick is to imagine that you're simply chatting to someone.

2 Don't look down

Even if you decide to learn your speech off by heart, you will need to have some notes to refer to in case your mind goes blank in the heat of the moment. However, don't deliver your speech while hiding behind a quivering piece of paper or constantly staring downwards. Look down for a moment, look up and speak. Get into a rhythm of doing this throughout your speech.

3 Breathe properly

When people get nervous, they forget to breathe and so easily swallow their words; this can render a beautifully written speech nearly inaudible. You don't want to deliver your speech only to find that no one could actually hear what you were saying. An effective way to combat the mumbling menace is by breathing properly – take deep, rhythmic breaths, as this will pump oxygen into your blood and keep your brain sharp and alert. Check that you're audible by arranging beforehand for someone at the back of the room to signal when your voice isn't carrying or ask for feedback at the start of your speech.

4 Set a good pace

Gabbling is another thing people tend to do when they're nervous. To stop yourself talking too fast, write the word 'pause' at intervals through your notes, or if you are using cue cards, insert blank ones that will automatically cause you to slow down. If you do lose your place, it's best just to make a joke of it.

5 Time your jokes

Pause briefly after you make a joke to give people a chance to laugh, but keep jokes and anecdotes short so that if one doesn't work, you can move on quickly to the next. If your joke dies, don't despair. Turn the situation to your advantage by inserting a quip such as 'Only me on that one then', or look round at an imaginary assistant and say: 'Start the car!' 'Rescue lines' like these can earn you a chuckle from a momentarily awkward silence.

6 Remember to smile

Making a speech is supposed to be fun, so make sure you don't look utterly miserable when you're doing it. Smile! Think of something that makes you laugh before you start speaking to get yourself in the right mood. Body language is important too, so adopt a relaxed posture before you begin – no crossed arms or fidgeting.

7 Start strongly

Opening lines are important, because they grab the audience's attention and get you off to a good start. Something like: 'Ladies and gentlemen, they say speeches are meant to be short and sweet, so thank you and good night,' should help you to begin in style.

8 Think positively

Instead of seeing your speech as a formal ordeal, think of it as being a conversation between you and a lot of people you know and really like, or as a way of wishing two good friends well. Thinking positively about your speech and the reason why you are there will help you to deliver it with confidence and make the task seem less intimidating.

Remember that weddings are happy occasions and all the guests want to see everything go well, including your speech. Be assured, the audience is on your side, they're all rooting for you, so make the most of it and use their goodwill to boost your confidence.

To help calm your nerves, imagine your speech being over and everyone applauding. Imagine how you'll feel when you can sit down, relax and really enjoy the rest of the evening. By visualizing everything going well, you should gain even more confidence.

9 Convey your message

Think about the meaning of your speech while you're making it. Concentrate on the thoughts you want to convey and the message behind your words, rather than just reciting your notes, as this will help you to make your delivery much more expressive.

10 End with a toast

Round off your speech with a toast. This will give it a focus and provide something to work towards. After you make your toast, you can sit down when everyone else sits down, signifying a definite end to your speech.

Stage fright
It's only natural to be nervous. If you find that you're really scared when you begin, don't panic. Make a joke out of it instead. Lines like 'This speech is brought to you in association with Imodium' or 'I was intending to speak but my tongue seems to be welded to the roof of my mouth' should raise a laugh and will help to get the audience on your side. One completely bald father of the bride started off on a high note by remarking: 'As you can see, I've been so worried about making this speech, I've been tearing my hair out.'

Wedding speech checklist

Once you've agreed to speak

- Start thinking about research.
- Think about the audience. Your speech will have to appeal to a wide range of people.
- Find out who'll be among the guests so that your material appeals and you don't cause offence.
- Ask friends and family for funny stories/embarrassing pictures that you can build into your speech.
- Keep your speech in the back of your mind. You never know when you might pick up a some juicy material.
- Keep a notebook to hand to jot down ideas.
- Speak to someone who's been a wedding speaker before and find out what not to do.
- Decide on the kind of speech you want. Will you need any props or visual aids or any equipment?

The build-up

- Think about the structure. Would the speech be better broken down into manageable chunks/themes?
- Does your speech do what it's supposed to do? Is it funny, affectionate and charming without being offensive?
- Have you included everything you need to say in your speech?
- Gather all the props/presentation aids you'll need and make sure you know how to use them.
- Build in time to practise your speech – the better rehearsed you are, the more confident you'll be, and the more everyone will enjoy it, yourself included.

Only a week to go

- Use a tape recorder or video camera to record yourself.
- Rope in an audience of friends to practise on.
- Be sure to practise your speech with any props you plan to use – winging it on the day is not a good bet.
- Time your speech; aim to keep it to around five minutes.
- Don't forget to allow time for reading out messages from absent friends and family.
- Write your speech in note form on cue cards, even if you intend to commit it to memory.
- Think positively about your speech and it will feel like less of an ordeal.
- Visualize your speech being over and everyone applauding as it will help to give you confidence and calm your nerves.
- Remember the audience is on your side – you'll be able to use their goodwill to boost your confidence.

The big day

A few last pointers to help your speech go smoothly:

- Try to relax and take it easy.
- Try not to look for Dutch courage in the bottom of your wine glass – you'll do your speech more harm than good!
- Keep busy with your other duties; this will help you to focus, and keep away those pre-speech nerves.
- Have your notes with you, even if you've committed your speech to memory. If your mind goes blank or you feel yourself veering off the point, at least you can refer to them, to get back on track.
- End your speech with a toast – it will give you something to work towards and be a clear signal that your bit is over.

great
speech
material

Inspiration for your speech

No matter what you plan to say, or for how long you intend to take the floor, it is essential that your speech has a good framework. In the pages that follow you will find good examples of opening and closing lines, and useful sample snippets should you know what you want to talk about, but not how to phrase it. Using these various 'ingredients' for inspiration, you should be able to construct a winning format with a strong beginning and end, a clear message in the middle and perhaps the odd joke or one-liner thrown in for impact.

Should you find the task of writing a speech from scratch altogether too daunting, there are also a handful of full-length sample speeches for you to choose from (see pages 144–157). Each one has a distinctive format that you can easily adapt to mould your unique material into a cohesive shape. Opt for a humorous account of how the happy couple met, a glowing tribute to your true friend, the bride, or a sentimental blessing on the union of the two families. Follow our guide and you simply cannot fail.

Great opening lines

'Excuse me, but I'm a little nervous. Now I know what a Rowntree's jelly feels like.'

'Did anyone see that polar bear walk by just now? No? Shame, because they're such terrific ice-breakers.'

'They say good speeches are meant to be pithy, although what oranges have got to do with it, I don't know.'

Jokes and one-liners

One-liners

'Greg was always considered a handsome chap at college. He was fastidious about getting his beauty sleep – about 20 hours a day, usually.'

'Now he's married, Dom can really let himself go... oh, you already have!'

'As the Bible says: "Who so findeth a wife, findeth a good thing." Now when I look at Jane, I can't help thinking, what a complete understatement!'

Jokes

'Sam and Sally are like very different wines: Sally gets better with age, whereas Sam just gets drunk.'

'Paula is busy making their new home comfortable, although Mark told me he's quite happy with his chair in the King's Head.'

'How many bridesmaids does it take to change a light bulb? Five. One to yank it out of the socket and chuck it, and four to squabble over who's going to catch it.'

End well

'And so, without further ado, let me ask those of you who can still stand up to join me in a toast...'

'And so will everyone now please raise their glasses – and themselves...'

'And so, in the words of my ex-boyfriend, "I'm going to leave you now"'.

'That's all from me, except to say that, for those of you who've never given a speech at a wedding, if you get an audience half as generous as you lot, you'll enjoy every minute of it...'

'One final thought. Always listen carefully to your partner's advice, so that when things go wrong you can say, "I told you so"!'

About the bride

Over the next 16 pages, we'll be offering you sample snippets on various topics, starting off here with the bride, that should cover all the bases you need to make your speech the best it can be.

One in a million

'Today I've been doing my duty as chief bridesmaid – and it's been great fun. But for years, Laura [the bride] has been doing her duty as best friend. She's comforted me when I've been sobbing my eyes out over various losers, and she's congratulated me when I've been promoted. We've shopped till we've dropped together, shared tonnes of chocolate and what must have been hundreds of bottles of wine. In all that time, Laura has been unfailingly kind, funny, generous and altogether one in a million. Tom, I'm sure you know it already, but let me say it again. You are a very, very lucky man.'

Daddy's girl

'When we were growing up, Mr Robinson was always everyone's favourite dad. We all looked up to him, especially Hannah [the bride]. I want to take this opportunity, Mr Robinson, to say "thank you" for your hospitality. Hannah is a wonderful girl. She's a good friend, a fine colleague and she's going to be a great wife. I'm sure she'd agree that all these things are a credit to you.'

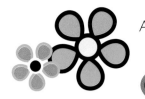

'Sarah's dad is truly a man of many talents. In fact, during the time I've known him, he's been Sarah's chauffeur, banker, agony aunt, secretary and occasionally personal shopper. I'm sure that now Sarah and John [the bride and groom] are married he's looking forward to a peaceful retirement.'

'Georgia [the bride] and her dad have always been close, and Max has been a tower of strength in the run up to the wedding. Never has a man endured so many conversations about flowers, veils, shoes, dresses and canapés. And all this without falling asleep once.'

She wears the trousers

'I first met Clare [the bride] when we both joined the Brownies at the age of six, and I can honestly say she is the bossiest person I've ever had the pleasure of knowing. How many girls aged seven would insist they knew better than Brown Owl how to light a fire? She proved it later, of course, when she managed to set fire to the chemistry labs.'

'Who else could the school have chosen to be head girl? Frankly, Jane [the bride] was acting like head girl from the moment she set foot in the door. The teachers didn't stand a chance – they couldn't get a word in edgeways. I must say I think Harry is coping remarkably well. YOU CAN TAKE THE EARPLUGS OUT NOW, HARRY!'

About the bride – from the sister of the bride or groom

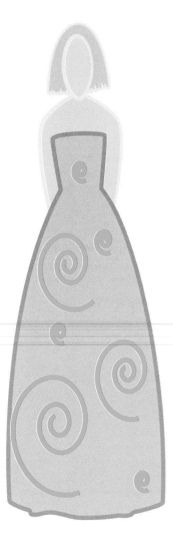

My sister

'As Marianne's younger sister, I have some advice for the groom. Peter [the groom], always treat Marianne [the bride] with respect. Never forget to listen to her opinions and value her contribution to your marriage. Never forget that she hates milk in her coffee, that she loves roses and can't stand classical music. And above all – and I speak from bitter experience – never, ever borrow her mascara without asking.'

'I think that perhaps because I'm Emily's big sister, I sometimes worry about her. But not today. Emily [the bride] has definitely found the right man in Edward [the groom] and I'm happy and proud to be their chief bridesmaid.'

'Ever since she was small, my sister Stella [the bride] has had a reputation for being a bit fussy about her clothes. As the chief bridesmaid who helped her get ready this morning, all I can say is that I need a drink – and I need it now!'

Sister act

'It feels like I've known Hattie [the bride] all my life. Actually, I have known Hattie all my life because for those of you who don't know, I'm her sister, and when I was born, Hattie had been in the world for a while already. Sibling loyalty means I'm not allowed to say exactly how many years, but it's a number between six and eight. And since I'm 24...

'So you can understand that when Brian [the groom] suggested that my speech contain some juicy anecdotes from Hattie's early life, I replied that the juicy bits had to start from her seventh birthday. He looked a bit disappointed, so I suspect he wanted some stories about how she used to cry and kick her legs about when she was having her nappy changed. Sorry, Brian – you'll have to get your kicks elsewhere.'

Older and wiser

'Joanne [the bride] is as perfect an elder sister as you could wish for. She's kind, she's understanding, she always has plenty of cash on her. She has been a shoulder to cry on for me.

'I remember once coming home from being stood up yet again by some spotty sixth-former, and she explained at great length that men were all good-for-nothings (actually she used a different word from that) and we women should never, but never, go anywhere near them. Lucky for Tim [the groom] that she didn't heed her own advice!'

A shining example

'I know that as the chief bridesmaid, my job is to tell you lots of stories about Donna's [the bride] misspent youth hanging out with dodgy lads at funfairs, halls and so on... a kind of best woman's speech. But as you know, Donna didn't have a misspent youth and has never been near a dodgy bloke in her entire life.

About the groom

When he was a kid

'Lucy [the bride] and I first met Simon [the groom] at playschool. She was the only girl he'd allow in the Wendy house and he was the only boy she'd allow to play with her on the water table. It was obviously love at first sight.'

'Suzie [the bride], Mike [the groom] and I all went to the same school, which means I've had the dubious pleasure of seeing Mike in a cagoule. He was the sort of kid other boys looked up to. Whether it was his multi-function utility belt or his animal-print desert boots that first caught Suzie's eye, I've yet to discover.'

My brother

'As you probably all know, the groom is, in fact, my brother. Quite what attracted Sara [the bride] to my childhood tormentor I'll never know. All I can say is if her ideal man burps, farts, swears, smells and snores, then she's found Mr Right.'

'When Polly [the bride] first started going out with my brother, I had mixed emotions. Here was my best friend, the person with whom I'd laughed, cried, shared secrets, watched soppy movies, shopped till we dropped and eaten copious amounts of chocolate with. And he was mad about Polly!'

'I don't feel that I'm losing a brother, any more than I feel I'm losing my best friend. The fact that two of the most valuable people in my life have fallen in love just fills me with great joy. Knowing them as well as I do, I'm confident that their love will only grow and flourish further as the years go by.'

Not squeaky clean

'Tanya [the bride] always said that she liked a bit of rough, but nothing prepared me for the first time I met Joe [the groom]. He'd just got back from work on the building site and was covered, head to toe, in all kinds of muck. His hair was stuck on end, his face was covered in dust, his clothes were caked in mud and his hands were black. This was going to be difficult. How could I possibly pretend to her that this scruff in front of me was an Adonis? But when he started talking, it all fitted into place. His charm, his humour, his compassion and his generous spirit shone through. And as you can all see today, he's not bad looking when he scrubs up, either.'

Going places

'When Bob [the groom] and I were little, I lost count of the number of times a grown-up remarked, "He's going places, that Robert." Secretly jealous, I used to laugh to myself that the only place Robert was likely to go was jail. But adolescent rivalry aside, I can see that the adults were right (as always) and Bob has indeed done very well for himself. There's the fantastic job, his unique physique, his world-beating collection of beer mats and now, of course, his perfect wife.'

About the families

Heartfelt thanks

'As chief bridesmaid I know it's my duty to get horribly drunk and stare in wonder and envy at the gorgeous bride we see here before us, while wondering when it'll be my turn. But before that happens, I'd like to say an enormous thank you to both sets of parents for making today happen and giving such a splendid party to mark the joining together of Lauren and Matthew [the bride and groom]. Additionally, Lauren's Auntie Carol also deserves a huge thank you for allowing this wonderful marquee to be pitched in her garden, and welcoming us all so generously. But most of all: Lauren you're my best friend and I want to thank you so much for the years of friendship as well as for choosing me to be your chief bridesmaid. It's been an incredible honour and I've loved every minute of it.'

Coming together

'Being at Sally and George's [the bride and groom's] wedding is a real "friends reunited" experience. There are people here tonight who haven't been together since we did our 'A' levels. It takes me back to the days of big hair, cocktails and Wham! songs – well, I'll definitely be requesting "Club Tropicana" later and I hope you'll join me for a boogie.'

'Seeing Harriet's and Paul's [the bride and groom] families together is an interesting experience. I can certainly see where they both get their brains and good looks from, not to mention their limitless capacity for partying.'

'As some of you may know, Ella and Anthony [the bride and groom] met when we were all working together, and it's great to see that so many people from our old office have turned up here today. We'll have to get together round the photocopier for a good gossip later on.'

Great mums

'Gill's mum has always been a special mum, and not just to Gill [the bride]. Whenever us kids were in trouble, it was always Gill's mum we turned to. She's always been there to sort out no end of problems, from cut knees to broken hearts. She's no different today. Even at the hen night, she was busy making sure we all got home safely in taxis from the nightclub, and let me tell you, there aren't many mums who can strut their stuff on the dance floor like she can!'

'As chief bridesmaid, I would just like to say a special thank you to Justine's mum. Justine and Jamie [the bride and groom] will tell you they organized the whole thing, but we all know what hopeless liars they are! Justine's mum has been the inspiration and the guiding light for much of what has happened today, not to mention chief-shoulder-to-cry-on when the bridesmaids' dresses didn't fit and my little nephew Jake decided to add some colour to the veil with his new felt-tips!'

The hen party

'In true best-friend style, I offered to do the driving for the hen party, which meant I had to stay sober. At the beginning, I felt I'd made a mistake – Clare [the bride] was having such a good time, letting her hair down and teasing the barmen. But at 3 in the morning, with Clare hanging round my neck telling me she loved me for the 10th time, I knew I had in fact made the right decision. [To the bride] And how long did it take to recover? Oh, that's right, it was a whole day before Clare was propping up the bar again!'

'There are not many who can claim to have been chief bridesmaid three times over, but there you have it. Of course it is flattering, but a real test of the imagination when it comes to arranging yet another hen party. I was lucky with Helen [the bride]. Early on in our friendship, I was aware that it did not take much to get her tipsy, and that she was no stranger to a touch of amnesia. On the night, I took her to the pub for a warm-up drink before meeting the other girls.

Six pints later, I was tucking her up in bed. The next morning, in answer to the question I knew was coming, I regaled Helen with an elaborate story of how we wined and dined at her favourite restaurant (the waiter couldn't take his eyes off her), before climbing into the back of a powder-pink stretch limo (champagne on tap) and danced the night away at Roxy's. She looked radiant, was the belle of the ball and had a truly fantastic time. And that is the story I'm sticking to!'

'I want to thank the girls who came on the hen trip – proof that you really cannot beat true friendship. Every year at school Susan [the bride] would plan a skiing trip that never happened. We'd all indulge her, saying 'sure, count me in', but knowing full well that, one way or another, we would not have to commit. It became a bit of an in-joke in the end and I know Susan often felt disappointed in us. When it came to arranging the hen party, skiing was the obvious choice. All five girls agreed to it and we relished making the arrangements in the utmost secrecy – thanks to John [the groom] Susan was utterly clueless. How we sniggered among ourselves along the way. Of course, we had a great time, but the best bit of all was when we revealed our plans to Susan – a moment I will never forget and one that fills me with real pride. It is difficult to describe the emotion of that moment, but let's just say it was well worth the wait.'

Absent friends

Thanking children

'When Alfie [page-boy] brought his pet frog to the wedding rehearsal, I thought he was going to be trouble. It took some doing to persuade him to leave the frog at home today – we both agreed it wasn't quite his scene – and I was worried about what Alfie might bring instead. But when I met him, and indeed all three of today's attendants this morning, with their best clothes on, their hair all smoothed down, and saw the serious expressions on their proud little faces, I knew we were going to have a good day. And they did not let me down. They really enjoyed being such an important part of the show and I think they deserve a round of applause.'

They couldn't be here

'You may have noticed that our dear friend Theresa is not here today to perform her usual role of hand-holder and general calming influence over proceedings. I can assure you, however, that she has a more than adequate excuse for missing the celebrations as she gave birth to a lovely baby boy, Josh, just four days ago. Look's like it'll be a hard day's night for all of us!'

Bereavement

'A wedding is not only a happy celebration but also a time to remember the people who are important in your life. And so let us all pause for a moment and say a silent prayer for all those here today who are missing loved ones, especially [give names if appropriate].'

'I was going to share the job of chief bridesmaid with Claire's childhood friend Alice. Alice had been seriously ill for some time, however, and sadly she passed away last month. Everyone who knew her will always remember the incredible zest for life she had and her boundless energy. And I know that right now, she's looking down and saying: "Just get on with it girl, and make sure you grab the last bottle of champagne"!'

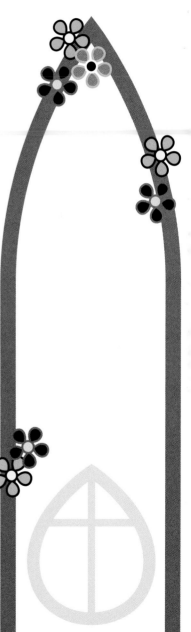

About the relationship

'These two have known each other since they were children. Even then there was quite a spark between them – although that's probably because Angela [the bride] liked to use Rick [the groom] as a human guinea pig in her science experiments...'

'They've known each other since Clara [the bride] went up to Ben [the groom] in the student union bar and asked him to hold her pint while she went to the loo. He fell in love on the spot there and then.'

'They've known each other since they bumped into one another at the launderette while at college. A perfectly normal way to meet someone, I suppose. Made remarkable only because that was the only day, in the three years that he was at uni, that Rob [the groom] went anywhere near a launderette.'

'The happy couple have known each other ever since they bumped into one another in the high street of Anna's home town. A romantic way to meet, I guess, except Anna [the bride] was in her car and Louis [the groom] was on his bike at the time. Ouch!'

'Dan [the groom] is determined that the honeymoon, which he has organized, will be truly romantic. He's planning walks on deserted beaches, downing cocktails and sampling the local cuisine. It's a secret, so I won't give too much away. Except to say that the cycle shop's done really well this month...'

'I wouldn't say the groom is romantic but I did hear he presented his lovely bride with three dozen roses and chocolates in bed on St Valentine's Day. Unfortunately the chocolate melted on to the sheets, which killed the mood a little...'

'We all know Phil [the groom] likes to take risks and he's already told me how, on the flight to their honeymoon, he's planning to do something naughty in the loo. Honestly, Phil, smoking's very bad for you!'

'I wouldn't say the bride and groom were particularly romantic. Instead of a flash engagement ring, they decided to buy something for the flat. In fact it's only because her parents came to the rescue that you're not currently being addressed by the dishwasher!'

Making a marriage last

Marriage is like...

'A good marriage is like a good novel. It has you hooked from day one, it's awe-inspiring, impossible to put down and you never want it to end.'

'A loving marriage is much like a fingerprint. It identifies who you are and stays with you for ever.'

'Marriage is like a cocktail: at its best it can leave you feeling like dancing in the street and singing from the rooftops. Sometimes it comes with fireworks and sometimes with a paper umbrella. Hmmm.'

My secret

'When Jan [the bride] and I were growing up, we often used to wonder which of the two of us would get married first. Who would have believed that it would turn out to be me? And so, as chief bridesmaid, I thought I'd share my secret with you for a successful marriage. The trick is to treat your man like you'd treat a mushroom. Keep him in the dark for as long as possible and he'll flourish.'

When the chips are down

'Today is about celebrating the love between Erica and Gary [the bride and groom]. Apart from the mystery of how she got that bruise on her hen night, there are no secrets between them. But in time there will inevitably be lows as well as highs, and when these darker times happen, it's important to focus on the reason you're together. Whenever things get tough, remember today, and everything that brought you to this moment.'

Communication

'As in any marriage, communication is one of the main reasons that Simon and I are still together. On our wedding day, happily married friends and relatives all emphasized to us the importance of talking things through and thinking things over, to make our life together as strong as possible. And I can honestly say that the advice rang true: communication is the key to our happy marriage. I talk and Simon listens.'

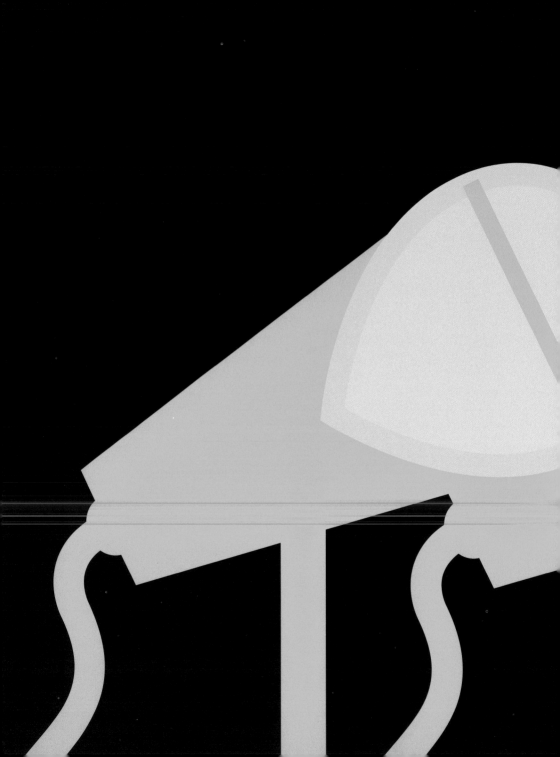

sample
speeches

Sample speech 1
Our student days

'Nicola [the bride] and I go back a long way – we met as happy-go-lucky students at Newcastle Uni.

'The fact that Nicola is here today in all her wedding finery is a scientific miracle. Having spent our formative student years living together in a condemned house from hell, it's a wonder that we survived at all – let alone finished the course, got jobs and found boyfriends. Our life there was a constant battle against the mould in the bathroom, an unidentified fungus underneath the kitchen sink, an enormous spider that didn't want to stay out, however much washing down the plughole we did, and to top it all the wiring must have been illegal.

'Tony [the groom], if you'd seen us back then, I doubt you would have been so fast to pop the question. Just so everyone has an idea, I've brought some pictures [hands out photocopies] so you can see for yourselves: the rubber gloves, the cleaning products, the scrubbing and mini-electrocutions – oh, the toll it took on our skin and hair, not to mention our fashion sense!

'That hairstyle of Nicola's [pointing to one picture in particular] was not at the hands of a student from the local salon... in fact, the plug socket in her bedroom kept giving little shocks through the hairdryer. I think the fuzzy look is not as strong a look now, and I'm sure her hairdresser would give that style a wide berth.

'Tony, we all know Nic is a great cook, but where did she get her international culinary inspiration? Well, we ordered a fair amount of local takeaways – Indian,

Chinese, Thai, Vietnamese, Greek, Turkish etc., etc. – since the kitchen was either stinking of bleach or recaptured by the mould. Unlike today, back then takeaways did not deliver and many a time, Nic would pop round the corner to collect our dishes of the day in her pyjamas or nightie – with a coat on top, well sometimes anyway. But one winter's evening, she was trundling back from the local Indian restaurant only to find when she reached our door that she'd forgotten her keys! Well, the guys in our local pub had a field day, since she had to wait there for me to come back. All this eating out malarkey also probably explains why she has an aversion to washing up, but you've probably gathered that by now, Tony.

'Another thing, Tone: is she still a bit security conscious? Does she still have a habit of double-checking the doors and making sure the windows are all shut when she goes into the back garden? Thought so! Hardly surprising since we had three break-ins in the first year – although they couldn't find anything worth nicking.

'But we came through it all together, me and Nicola, and it's made our friendship (and our stomach linings) all the stronger. So when she invited me to be her chief bridesmaid I felt honoured – almost as happy as the day we moved out of that house from hell. Truth to be told, I have missed you ever since, Nic, and I'm proud to stand here and raise a toast to Tony and his new housemate: May your new life together be nothing like ours was!'

Sample speech 2
The bride's Top 10 tunes

'Louise [the bride] is a karaoke queen, and if she had her way she'd spend the rest of her life singing into a hairbrush in front of the mirror. In consultation with her dancefloor divas, I've drawn up a private inventory of her most listened-to records and compiled a Top 10. Here's what they say about her.

'Abba's *Dancing Queen*. To say that Louise loves dancing is an understatement. Not long after we met she won a break-dancing award in the local youth centre championships. Get her in the right mood and she'll do a repeat performance...

'*Who Do You Think You Are*, by the Spice Girls. Louise is a force to be reckoned with. Loyal to the last, she'll fight all your battles and never let you down. Just don't ever nick her Hobnobs, though.

'Kylie Minogue's *Fragile*. After a couple of vodkas, Louise has been known to take to the sofa for most of the day. To revive her, bring her pints of water and cook her a big fry-up first thing.

'Elvis' *All Shook Up*. Ever been in the car while Lou's driving? You want to make sure your seatbelt is very secure, there's no fizzy pop in the back and you've not eaten too much before you get in. Take the bus is my advice.

'*Freak Like Me*, by the Sugababes. I'm referring of course to her famous temper. I don't need to remind close friends and family that the Incredible Hulk has nothing on this girl when your cross her. Simon, you have been warned!

'Razorlight's *Golden Touch.* I'm not saying she's led a charmed life, but it hasn't been without a big share of good luck. From winning at bingo (I've witnessed this twice) to getting a good price on her first house, bagging cheap air fares and always knowing just where to get the real bargains in the sales, stick with Louise if you want a good deal!

'Lily Allen's *Smile.* I dare anyone to last more than a couple of minutes in Lou's company without finding something to smile about. And sometimes, Lou, we swear it's not intentional but we're laughing with you, not at you (at least that's the party line, isn't it Simon?).

'*Better Man*, by Robbie Williams. It's tough on a girl when your best friend moves out of your life and into someone else's, but Lou's always had impeccable taste (modest, aren't I?) – and Simon is no exception to that rule. I feel like I gained a best friend, instead of losing one.

'Sarah Brightman's *Starship Trooper.* Lou's Mum told me that she always had her head in the clouds when she was little, but I would say that in choosing Simon, she's made a very grounding decision. Guys, I hope your skies are always blue, and your sun's always shining.

'*The Time of My Life,* by Bill Medley and Jennifer Warnes. Louise, I know today is one you'll remember forever – and now, will everyone please raise their glasses in wishing Lou and Simon the time of their lives!'

Sample speech 3

Almost Bridezilla

'I'll start off by reading the Webster's definition of Bridezilla: *"bride-zil-a* n. Horrific, bulging-eyed bride prone to screaming spells and spontaneous fits of hysterical rage. Bridezillas are known to drop blows over seating charts, get bug-eyed at the mere mention of carnations and view hurling champagne at their wedding planners as a form of ritualistic test".

'Well you may think that that version is a bit extreme but organizing weddings can bring out an unknown side to a person. We know Jane [the bride] as being so organized and particular – she puts the rest of us to shame. The hotel manager just told me he lost the original booking for this reception because they don't usually keep bookings made more than five years ago!

'As you know, or perhaps if you come from Peter's [the groom] side of the family, you don't know: Jane has a bit of a reputation in our family for...um, how can I say this politely?...wanting everything to be 'just so'.

'I thought you might like to see the instructions that Jane gave me about how the bouquet should be [bring out computer print-out that falls concertina-like from your hands to the floor]. The colours of the flowers come from one of those painting machines. We had to make three trips to the shop to get the right blue. And, I bet I don't even get to catch the bouquet later!

'Well, it's quite right I suppose to want things just so, especially on such an important day, and Jane does have such an eye for detail. I did notice, for example, that the two little models of the bride and groom on top of the fantastic wedding cake had been straightened slightly between the time I arrived here and the time we sat down for lunch. Now, who could have done that, I wonder?

'When we were choosing the dress – and I kid you not – we looked at 42 different wedding-dress catalogues. 42! In the time it took Jane to choose the patterns for the bridesmaids' dresses, England could have won the World Cup. Well, perhaps not won it, but definitely reached the quarter-finals.

'We've had such fun planning this wedding but I have to say that I was a little scared on a few occasions when the hitherto unseen Bridezilla exploded onto the scene. The first time I witnessed this 'extra' side to Jane was when the ribbons for the favours were just all wrong – "too ribbony" was the actual quote; the last was when I tried to help organize some karaoke for her hen party.

'[to the bride] For all your quirkiness, I love you Jane: you're my best friend and I wish you and Peter all the best in your future together.

'To the happy couple!'

Sample speech 4
Holidays from hell

'Don't worry – I promise I'll keep this short! But as Karen's [the bride] chief bridesmaid, I couldn't let this occasion pass without saying a few words. Those of you who know me may say that I can't let any occasion pass without speaking, but that's another story...

'Now Karen has been my best friend since we were in the Infants, and even at that young age she dreamt of faraway lands and the handsome prince who would take her there. Well, we've both had to kiss a few frogs in our time but I'm delighted to see that she's finally found her prince in Steve [the groom].

'When Karen asked me to be her bridesmaid I was of course honoured and delighted to accept – I've known Steve for a long time and can't imagine anyone better for her. But I have to admit that I had a few misgivings when she told me her news, and not for reasons you might think either.

'My concern centred on the fact that surely a wedding means a honeymoon? The holiday of a lifetime? With Karen?!!

'For those of you – and that would seem to include you Steve! – who are now looking at me oddly, let me explain. When the handsome prince still hadn't shown up a few years ago, Karen and I made a pact to concentrate on the faraway lands for a while. We have now been on five holidays together and, well Steve, whatever happens I can promise you it won't be dull.

'Maybe she's just been practising on me to prepare for the perfect holiday with you. I certainly hope so, for your sake.

'Certainly I think we've covered most eventualities on our

travels – two weeks of diarrhoea, two lost passports (one stolen), one broken leg, three missed flights (yes, that's *three* missed flights), an incident involving a ferret and some nail scissors, two lost suitcases and a night behind bars (mistaken identity, but still a good story).

'I would like to point out that all of the above incidents involved Karen and not myself – you may know her as a responsible paediatric nurse but give the girl a plane ticket and a passport and all hell breaks loose. Why do you think I was so keen on you two honeymooning in Norfolk?

'Don't get me wrong – I don't know what I am going to do for entertainment now that she has found a new travelling companion, and I am sure the pair of you will have a wonderful time wherever you go. Just make sure you double-check that insurance policy before you leave…

'I would just like to finish by saying that despite the mishaps, or maybe even because of them, Karen has always been the best friend and travelling companion through life's ups and downs that anyone could ever hope for. I am sure you will join me in wishing her and her new husband every happiness as they embark on their wedded journey together and set off into the future. So, now refill your glasses and please raise them once more: 'For Karen and Steve, the bride and groom!'

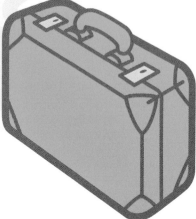

Sample speech 5

Ten things you didn't know about the bride

'It's wonderful to see so many of you here tonight to celebrate Kate and Tom's [the bride and groom] wedding. We've just heard all about Tom's strange foibles, but even though I'm sure many of you here think you know Kate well, I'm here to reveal some hidden depths to the girl...

'First, let me set the scene. As elder sister to the bride I think it's fair to say I know her pretty well. Like all sisters our relationship has been through a rocky patch when we were younger (I seem to remember that lasted approximately 15 years), but in recent times she has come to understand at last how great I truly am.

'So while I really don't want to rock the boat, this is my one chance to get my own back for all those times I got the blame and she got away with it. I can see all the older siblings in the room nodding knowingly, so I'll carry on.

'I've been thinking about this speech for a while now and eventually came up with my Top 10 list of things that I bet you don't know about my baby sister. None of them are bad things – we all know she doesn't have a bad bone in her body – but there may be a few surprises – especially for you Tom! So here goes...

1 'As a small child Kate was prone to eating slugs and can still be seen casting a longing look at anything that slimes and wriggles.
2 'Kate used to run my favourite teddy's paws under the hot tap if I didn't play with her.

3 'She'll never admit, but I know for a fact that her favourite film is *Christmas on Walton's Mountain*.

4 'She has always wanted six children (Tom, you don't look like you knew that one...).

5 'She scratches her neck when she's not telling the truth.

6 'She still sucks her thumb when she thinks no one's looking.

7 'Her first love was Nik Kershaw.

8 'After her first date with Tom, she called me up and told me she knew she was going to marry him.

9 'After her second date, she knew she wasn't.

10 'She has never been as happy as she has been since she met Tom.

'I may have cheated on the last one as I'm sure it's no surprise to anybody here that Kate and Tom are made for each other. I, for one, am just glad she finally got over that Nik Kershaw obsession.

'Corny as it may sound, I really couldn't be happier than I have been today watching my little sis' marry Tom. He's been close to our family for some years now, something that would probably have seen off lesser men. It seems that as well as having impeccable taste in women he's got courage too. I just hope he's got the patience for all those kids...

'So, ladies and gentleman, for one final time this evening, can I please ask you to raise your glasses to Kate and Tom, the bride and groom.'

Sample speech 6
Online obsessions

'Ladies and gentleman, I am honoured that Daisy [the bride] has asked me to be her bridesmaid, and a little amazed that she has allowed me my own speaking slot on her big day.

'Over the past few weeks, I've thought a lot about what I should say tonight. I could have played it safe and focused on the happy couple and the wonderful life I am sure they will have together. Somehow though, it didn't seem quite right to let the day pass without mentioning the other love of Daisy's life. No, not the usual George Clooney or chocolate – I'm talking about her computer.

'Daisy's online obsession began a few years ago now when she discovered ebay. Suddenly she could shop for bargains day and night – what could be more perfect? This got her thinking. Maybe she could indulge another of her passions – gossiping – without actually leaving her seat either. One thing lead to another and, as far as I can see, Daisy now spends most of her days (and nights) showing off on MySpace, sending us all her favourite YouTube clips and extending her friends network on Facebook.

'Indeed, if you were thinking she looked a little distracted today that's probably because she hasn't logged on for at least six hours (though I wouldn't be surprised if there was a BlackBerry hidden among those petticoats).

'Anyway, as part of my research for today, I decided to give her friends in Facebook a quick 'poke' and run a poll to find out if they really are her friends or not. A lot of you are here with us now and here are the results:

- '96 per cent think that Daisy and Mike are a perfect match. I'm just looking to see if any of the 4 per cent are here today...
- '25 per cent think she drinks too much
- '45 per cent think she doesn't drink enough
- '15 per cent think she is prone to grumpiness (I need to check that figure – surely that can't be right?).

'Although it started out as a quick poll to get material for today, one thing that quickly became clear is how extremely popular Daisy is. I've known her for more than 20 years so that was no surprise to me, but it's no mean feat to have such a wide circle of friends when you never seem to leave the house.

'Computer-obsessive or not, I am privileged to be able to count Daisy among my closest friends and delighted that she has finally agreed to marry Mike and put him out of his misery. I just hope that the romantic beach hut in the Maldives has a wi-fi connection... All that remains for me to say now is to ask you all please to raise your glasses once more and toast the bride and groom.'

Index